TINNED FISH
PANTRY
COOKBOOK

TINNED FISH PANTRY

COOKBOOK

100 *Recipes from Tuna & Salmon to Crab & More*

SUSAN SAMPSON

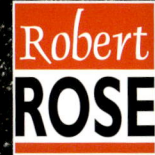

Tinned Fish Pantry Cookbook
Text copyright © 2021 Susan Sampson
Recipe photographs copyright © 2021 Ashley Lima
Cover and text design copyright © 2021 Robert Rose Inc.

Some of the recipes in this book were previously published in *200 Best Canned Fish & Seafood Recipes*, published in 2012 by Robert Rose Inc.

No part of this publication may be reproduced, stored in a retrieval system or transmitted, in any form or by any means, without the prior written consent of the publisher or a license from the Canadian Copyright Licensing Agency (Access Copyright). For an Access Copyright license, visit www.accesscopyright.ca or call toll-free: 1-800-893-5777.

For complete cataloguing information, see page 184.

Disclaimer
The recipes in this book have been carefully tested by our kitchen and our tasters. To the best of our knowledge, they are safe and nutritious for ordinary use and users. For those people with food or other allergies, or who have special food requirements or health issues, please read the suggested contents of each recipe carefully and determine whether or not they may create a problem for you. All recipes are used at the risk of the consumer.

We cannot be responsible for any hazards, loss or damage that may occur as a result of any recipe use.

For those with special needs, allergies, requirements or health problems, in the event of any doubt, please contact your medical adviser prior to the use of any recipe.

DESIGN AND PRODUCTION: Kevin Cockburn/PageWave Graphics Inc.
EDITOR: Kathleen Fraser and Gillian Watts
INDEXER: Gillian Watts
RECIPE PHOTOGRAPHER: Ashley Lima
ADDITIONAL PHOTOGRAPHS: © gettyimages.com, except page 20 © shutterstock.com
VINTAGE CANNED FISH LABELS (page 11): © Gulf of Georgia Cannery Society

COVER IMAGE: California Salmon Salad (page 80)
BACK COVER IMAGE: Tuna Pantry Pasta (page 158)

The publisher gratefully acknowledges the financial support of our publishing program by the Government of Canada through the Canada Book Fund.

Canada

Published by Robert Rose Inc.
120 Eglinton Avenue East, Suite 800, Toronto, Ontario, Canada M4P 1E2
Tel: (416) 322-6552 Fax: (416) 322-6936
www.robertrose.ca

Printed and bound in China

1 2 3 4 5 6 7 8 9 LEO 29 28 27 26 25 24 23 22 21

Contents

• • •

INTRODUCTION	9
A WORLD OF CANNED SEAFOOD	13
CANNED SEAFOOD FAQ	25
GETTING STARTED	31
SOUPS	45
SALADS	63
SANDWICHES & WRAPS	87
FISH BURGERS, FISH CAKES & MORE	111
CASSEROLES, PIES & CURRIES	129
PASTA, RICE & GRAINS	151
INDEX	185

INTRODUCTION

WHEN I FIRST told people I was writing a cookbook starring canned seafood, I heard a lot of jokes about slaving over a hot can opener and stocking up for civil emergencies. There is a certain snobbery surrounding tinned fish, but it also has fans in the millions. Trouble is, even devotees don't always know what to do with a can of fish or seafood, beyond mashing it up with mayo or tossing it into a casserole with condensed soup.

A couple of decades ago, as food editor at the *Toronto Star*, I opened a story file and scribbled "Start with a Can of Tuna" on the label. I never did write that story, as daily newspaper deadlines and food news got in the way. However, I remained convinced that a home cook could get creative with canned tuna and its cousins.

In 2012, Robert Rose published my *200 Best Canned Fish & Seafood Recipes*. Now I'm excited to introduce *Tinned Fish Pantry Cookbook: 100 Recipes from Tuna & Salmon to Crab & More*. This is a compact, current version of that original handy book. In these trying times, people are stocking up, sheltering at home and cooking from scratch. They are buying and relying on pantry staples. And what could be more reliable than versatile, shelf-stable, healthy canned fish? No wonder consumers have been whisking more canned fish and seafood off supermarket shelves during the pandemic.

In the kitchen, my repertoire ranges from haute to folksy. Fortunately, canned seafood is there to respond to my whims. It's easy to downscale or upscale recipes depending on the type of seafood I select. Tuna, for instance, runs the gamut from inexpensive water-packed fish to pricey belly fillets in extra virgin olive oil. When I crave a taste of crab, I can snack on a dip whipped up with a little can of flaky crab or wow guests with a refined salad starring white crabmeat chunks. I do love to get fancy. But as a working mother I also realize that the world is spinning too fast. It's tough to get weekday family meals on the table or stuff lunches into those brown bags late at night. That's when humble canned salmon comes to the rescue. When you're pressed for time or money, or isolating at home, it's nice to know you can raid the pantry.

Fresh seafood is dandy, but canned seafood is ready when you are. It's a speedy alternative to fast food. It's generally nutritious, economical and convenient. And a lot of varieties of seafood are interchangeable in recipes, so you can swap what you have on hand. Where appropriate, my recipes suggest such substitutions: look for the "Catch of the Day." So yes, enjoy fresh fish when you have it, along with the time to fuss with it and the money to pay for it. But feel free to use canned fish in situations that are less ideal — when you are in a hurry, when you are penny-pinching or when you have to customize dinner for those picky kids.

The key to cooking with canned seafood is this: treat it as a different species from fresh fish. The flavors and textures are different. Don't treat canned seafood as a sad second-class substitute. Don't try to turn it into something it's not. Instead, work with the differences. Handle it gently and remember that it has already been cooked during the canning process. The techniques and recipes in this book will help you make the most of canned seafood. Have fun experimenting.

— Susan Sampson

ALLY BRAND
GUARANTEE "ALLY" SALMON IS GUARANTEED TO CONSIST OF FRESHLY CAUGHT FINEST SELECTED FISH PACKED AT ITS BEST UNDER IDEAL CONDITIONS
ALLY BRAND
FANCY RED CUTLETS
SALMON
FANCY RED CUTLETS
HODGSON & CO. PTY. LTD.
SYDNEY, MELBOURNE, BRISBANE, ADELAIDE, WELLINGTON, (N.Z.)
PACKED IN ALASKA
CAPTAIN
TRADE MARK
EMPIRE
CAPTAIN BRAND
FINEST RED SOCKEYE
NET WEIGHT 7¾ OZS.
SALMON STEAK
PRODUCE
SALMON STEAK
FIRST GRADE SELECTED FRESH RED SOCKEYE SALMON CAUGHT IN SEASON
DISTRIBUTORS:
DOWNS DISTRIBUTING CO.LTD
SYDNEY, AUSTRALIA
PRODUCE OF CANADA
BLUE FLAKE
BLUE FLAKE
FANCY RED BLUEBACK
NET CONTENTS 15½ OZ.
PRINTED IN CANADA
SALMON
SHAFER-HAGGART LTD. VANCOUVER, CANADA.
Salmon
Silverlake BRAND
ZALM
POIDS NET 440 GRAMMES
PRODUIT DU CANADA
POIDS NET ÉGOUTTÉ 360 G.
SAUMON AU NATUREL
Silverlake BRAND

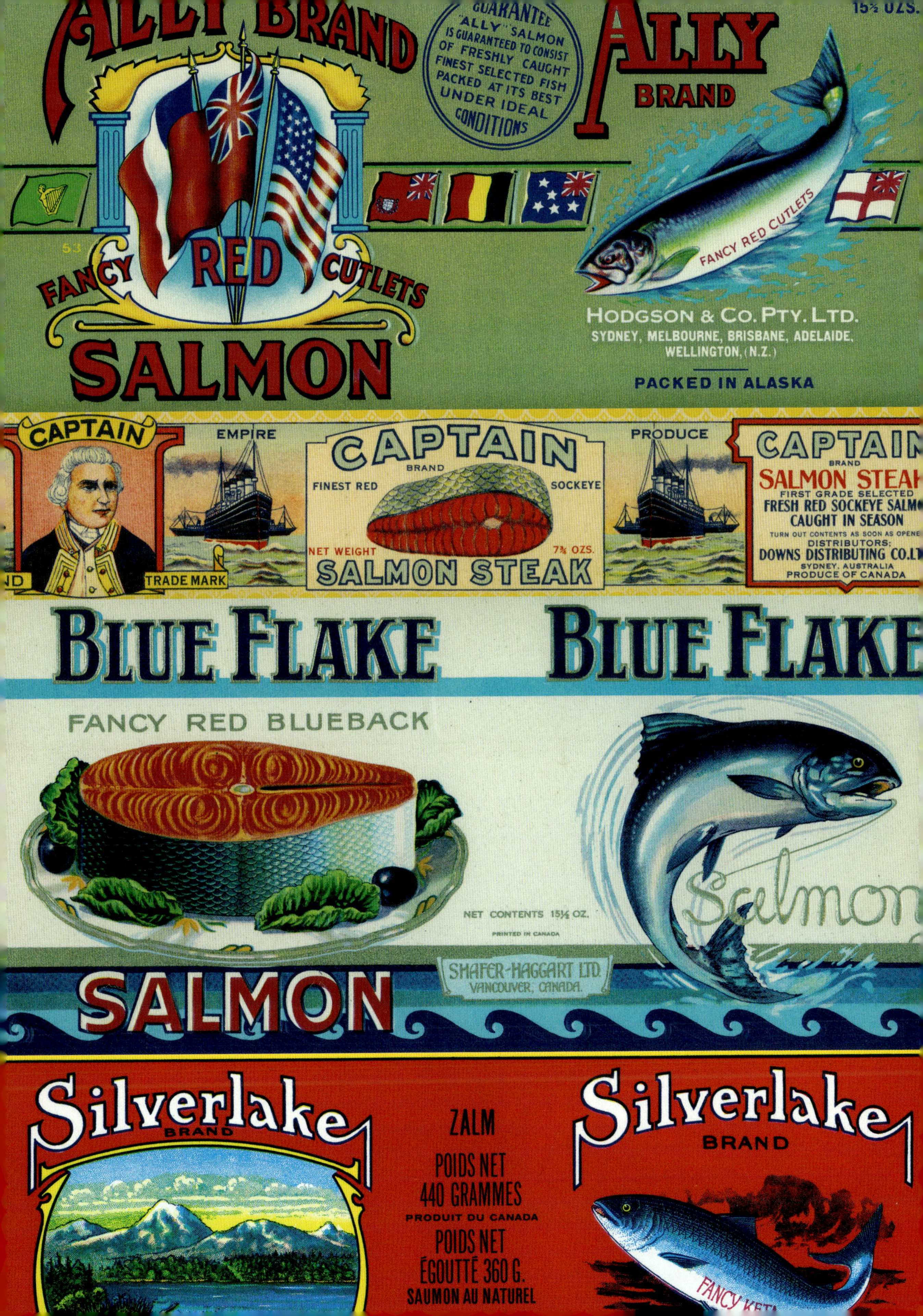

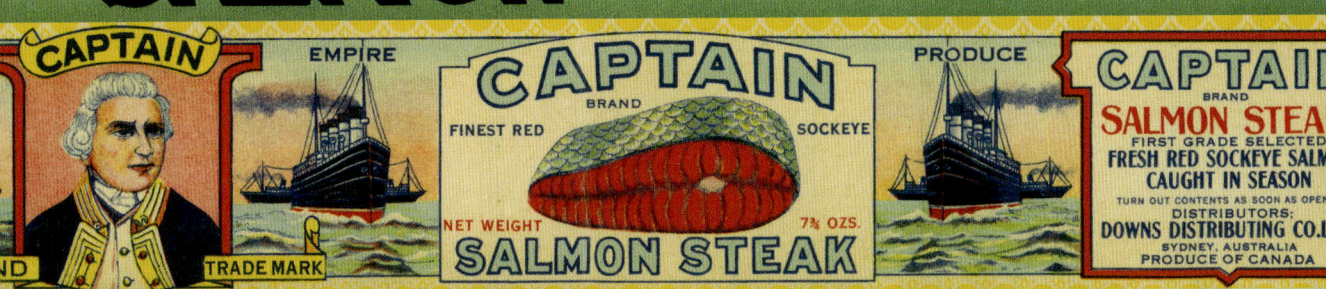

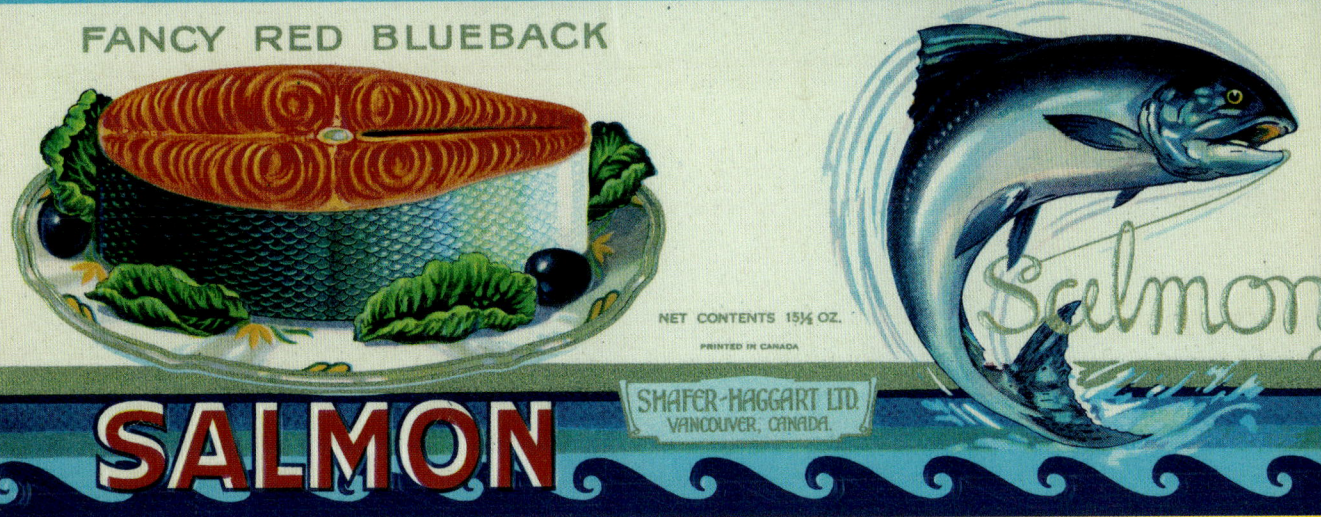

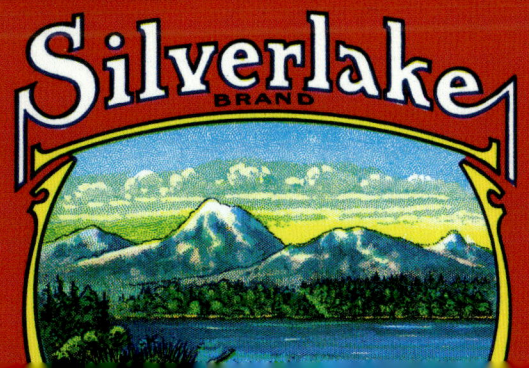

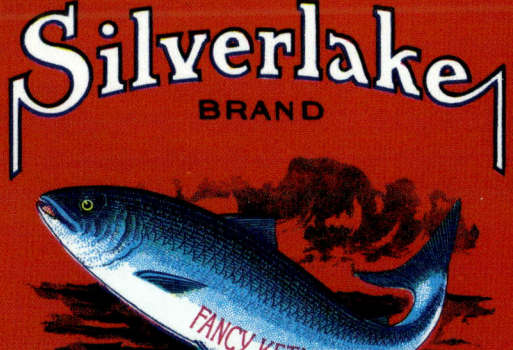

A WORLD OF CANNED SEAFOOD

CHOICES, CHOICES. From tuna to crab, many varieties of seafood are available in cans and tins, at a wide range of prices depending upon the species and quality. The seafood may be wild or farmed. It may be packed in water, oil, broth or a combination thereof, or simply in its own juices. It may be salted, smoked, spiced or swimming in sauce. It may be flaked or in fillets or skinless and boneless. It may have been canned in North America or imported from faraway places such as Thailand.

The recipes in this book feature the most readily available seafoods: tuna, salmon, sardines, anchovies, crab and clams. If you have a tin of any one of these ingredients in your pantry, you have the makings of a meal.

VARIATIONS AND SUBSTITUTIONS

Look for the "Catch of the Day" symbol. Each recipe in this book stars a specific seafood. I have also suggested variations for many of the recipes. For example, salmon can fill in for tuna, or vice versa; clams may fill in for crab. (Some recipes also include mackerel as a possible substitution.) This will help you work with whatever you have in the pantry. A lot of canned seafood is interchangeable in recipes, so don't be afraid to play around.

As popular, plentiful and familiar as canned seafood may be, however, consumers still look at the labels and get confused. The following guide to choosing and using canned fish and seafood should help.

TUNA

Tuna is the second most popular seafood in North America, after shrimp, and has a strong following in Europe. Although tuna is an everyday pantry item, shoppers faced with the array on supermarket shelves can get dizzy trying to figure out what kind to buy. Some labels are full of information while others are vague and puzzling.

TYPES OF CANNED TUNA

First of all, which species do you want? Chances are the tuna is albacore, yellowfin or skipjack, and the label will say the meat is white or light. Here's how to decode that information:

- Albacore is choice, meaning good quality or preferable. The proverbial chicken of the sea, it is prized for its firm, pale flesh and mild flavor. Albacore (also known as tombo or longfin tuna) is labeled "white tuna."
- Yellowfin and skipjack are classified as "light tuna" and cost less than albacore. Depending on your bias, they taste more flavorful or fishier than albacore. Skipjack is the smallest type of tuna but boasts the biggest market share. The majority of tuna eaten around the world is skipjack. Yellowfin (also known as yellowtail or ahi) is the largest of the commonly canned tunas. It has a better reputation than skipjack, thanks to its slightly milder flavor and lighter flesh.
- Two other light tunas that are sometimes canned are tongol and bigeye. Never say never, but you are unlikely to find bluefin tuna in a can. Sushi-makers fight over this expensive and endangered fish; it has the darkest, fattiest flesh.
- The bonito is a cousin of tuna; scientifically speaking, it belongs to the same family. If bonito is in the can, it must be labeled as such. Bonito has a strong flavor and high fat content. You can use it as you would tuna. Do not confuse bonito with bonito del norte, a term the Spanish may use to describe high-quality albacore tuna.

SOLID, CHUNKS OR FLAKES?

Canned tuna is also classified by the size of the chunks. You can get a loin, pieces of loin or the flakes that fall off when tuna is processed. The larger the chunks, the more expensive the tuna, because intact tuna is more attractive and has a better texture.

- Solid tuna is a single piece of loin. It is usually albacore but sometimes yellowfin.
- Chunk tuna consists of large pieces of fish. Chunks are usually yellowfin or skipjack but sometimes albacore.
- Flakes are just that. They range from albacore to bonito. The best are simply pieces that have flaked off albacore loins. The worst look dark, taste tinny, feel mushy and smell fishy.
- Grated or shredded tuna comes in uniform particles but must not be a paste. Decades ago it was used in cooking as you would use flakes, but today it is not commonly stocked in supermarkets. It may be used commercially or in prepared sauces or dips.
- Specialty items include tuna fillets packed in olive oil and, at high-end shops, belly tuna.

OTHER TUNA CHOICES

Tuna comes in shelf-stable tins, pouches and bottles. It can be packed in water, olive or other oils, or broth, or a combination thereof. Some premium tuna is smoked. All containers are shelf-stable.

The bestselling tuna is versatile middle-of-the-road chunk light tuna packed in water. Most consumers buy water-packed tuna to save money and calories. However, tuna packed in oil is richer and smoother, with a more concentrated flavor. If you are going to spend the calories, buy tuna in extra virgin olive oil. It is a healthier fat than refined vegetable or soybean oil.

USING CANNED TUNA

All types of canned tuna can be used in recipes in this book. However, some are better choices for certain recipes, and I've specified which. Generally speaking, use solid or larger-chunk tuna for salads, casseroles or curries. Buy chunk tuna or even flaked white tuna if you are going to mash it up in dips and the like. For cooked dishes, many people favor light tuna such as yellowfin or skipjack over albacore. (Not only is light tuna less expensive, it has a fuller flavor.) Because it costs more, save tuna in olive oil for green salads, sandwiches and pastas where it takes a starring role.

SALMON

Salmon is next on the list of popular canned fish. Wild Pacific sockeye and pink are the two most common kinds of canned salmon.

TYPES OF CANNED SALMON

- Pink salmon (also known as humpback) is the lightest, mildest and leanest species of salmon. Its flesh is soft and mild (or bland, depending on your taste). Pink salmon costs less than red sockeye.
- Sockeye's firm red flesh and rich taste make it the king of canned salmon. Sockeye has the second highest fat content of the popular salmon species. Premium sockeye may be labeled blueback, a moniker that refers to the color of its scales in salt water during the period when it is fattest and tastiest.

Three other species of Pacific salmon are usually sold fresh or smoked. However, they may also be canned. These are not available in all regions. If you want a specific type of salmon, you may have to shop for it online.

- Chinook is the largest and fattiest of the Pacific salmons, with velvety dark orange flesh rich in healthy omega-3 fats. It is also called king, blackmouth or spring salmon.
- The small coho (also known as silver salmon) is milder tasting and leaner than sockeye or chinook.
- The least expensive salmon is chum, also called keta, dog or calico salmon. It has lean, mild orange-pink flesh that tends to flake.

WHAT'S IN THE CAN?

Salmon is canned in its own juices or in water. The skin and soft bones are edible; the amounts vary from can to can, depending on the original size of the fish. Alternatively, you can buy boneless, skinless salmon in cans. The pieces are usually solid or chunks, but I have seen flaked salmon. Tinned smoked salmon is a premium product sold in specialty food shops or upscale supermarkets.

FARMED SALMON

Some of the salmon found in cans is Atlantic salmon. Since the collapse of the wild fishery, Atlantic salmon is almost always farmed. (Salmon farms are located on both the east and west coasts of North America. Some salmon is also farmed organically in Europe.) In contrast, most canned Pacific salmon is wild. To choose, check the label. It will usually specify Atlantic salmon or say "wild" — the latter being a marketing plus.

A WORLD OF CANNED SEAFOOD

USING CANNED SALMON

Any type of canned salmon can be used in the recipes in this book. For certain recipes the more expensive sockeye is a better choice than pink salmon. I generally prefer sockeye because it is redder and richer-tasting. But in most cases you can successfully substitute less expensive pink salmon.

SARDINES

What is a sardine? It is not a species but rather a marketing term. The name comes from the Mediterranean island of Sardinia, one of the first places sardines were canned. Today's sardines are immature soft-boned, oily saltwater fish that travel in schools by the millions. A canned sardine may be a juvenile pilchard, herring or sprat. Fish become sardines once they are crammed into a tin (like sardines, so to speak) with their peers.

Half a century ago, sardine canneries were bustling on both coasts of North America. Today sardines are a harder sell. Consumers' tastes have changed; many seem to object to the bold flavor, strong scent and humble reputation of sardines. That's too bad. Sardines are one of the healthiest canned fish choices for you and the environment — abundant, sustainable, low in mercury and full of calcium and heart-healthy oils. This is a good time to revive their reputation.

FISH SHE IS VERY SMALL

When buying sardines, the smaller the fish and the more in the tin, the higher the quality. All sardines are juvenile fish, but the youngest and smallest are more tender and milder. Hence the comical vintage motto from one manufacturer, "Fish she is very small."

TYPES OF TINNED SARDINES

Sardines are packed headless but whole, usually in vegetable or olive oil but sometimes in spring water to suit modern tastes. They may also be "slightly smoked," as one label describes it. Some sardines are labeled "silds," which are juvenile herrings. Small sardines may also be labeled "Jutlands." Also available are boneless, skinless sardines; they are firmer and less likely to fall apart in cooking. Besides the proverbial sardines on toast, these little fish are good in salads, sandwiches and pastas.

A WORLD OF CANNED SEAFOOD

Keep a special lookout for petite brislings in extra virgin olive oil. These sardines are the finest, tastiest and highest in omega-3 fats. Brisling sardines are usually the young of a specific species, called sprats, from icy northern waters. When smoked and preserved in oil, sprats go by their own name rather than being lumped under the sardine marketing banner. These petite, fatty, herring-like fish look pretty and taste deliciously smoky. They are tinier and more delicate-looking than standard sardines, with finer, bronzed skins and an appealing milder flavor yet firmer flesh. Sprats are a treat on their own with a spritz of lemon, but you can also use them to upscale any of the sardine recipes in this book or as substitutes for other smoked fish. Beware, though: they can be quite salty.

Also beware of those oversized (21 ounce/600 g) tins of salted sardines. The tins are very big and round and are labeled "salted sardines." Sardines and salt are the only two ingredients. These are not your grandma's easy-to-eat sardines on toast. Beheaded, smelly and packed in lots of coarse salt, they must be washed, gutted, deboned, filleted and cooked before you can use them.

ANCHOVIES

Anchovies are the little fish that could. The true anchovy is a fatty little Mediterranean fish related to the herring. But there are more than a hundred varieties of anchovy swimming in the world's oceans. Their salty, lip-smacking flavor has made them a vital kitchen ingredient since the ancient Romans used them to prepare a fermented sauce called garum. Today the anchovy is a secret ingredient that sneaks into all kinds of food to deliver pizzazz. Anchovies may be hidden in plain sight, in pasta or Caesar salad, or discreetly added to Worcestershire sauce or Vietnamese fish sauce. Anchovies fare worse with the public when they take on starring roles. The anchovies-on-pizza debate, for example, has undoubtedly been raging as long as there has been pizza.

TYPES OF TINNED ANCHOVIES

These tasty little fish come in tins or jars, usually flat but sometimes rolled. Unlike most canned fish, anchovies are not sterilized using heat (they'd turn to mush) and contain no artificial preservatives. Instead, anchovies are "semi-preserved" or "partially preserved" — cured using salt and oil. They are filleted, salted, packed in tins or bottles and then immersed in oil. Thus they are considered an "artisan" tinned fish.

Check labels and spring for the anchovies in extra virgin olive oil. The irresistible salty oil is a bonus in itself and can be used to enhance your anchovy dishes. Anchovies in extra virgin olive oil are available in supermarkets, in refrigerated cases near the seafood or deli offerings.

"Semi-preserved" equals semi-perishable, so keep unopened tins in a cool location; it's safest and simplest to store them in the fridge and keep track of the best-before date. Ideally, anchovies should be kept in a refrigerator at 41°F (5°C) or lower; under those conditions they should be good for six months. Once the tin is opened, the anchovies must be refrigerated; they will keep for about two months. Transfer them to a little storage tub and make sure they are submerged in oil. Don't be afraid to freeze stray anchovies if you must. Just wrap them individually in foil or plastic.

COOKING WITH ANCHOVIES

Before using anchovies, rinse and pat them dry to remove excess salt. Some cooks soak anchovies in water, milk or wine to soften them. Anchovies can be pounded into a paste, mashed with a fork or dissolved in hot olive oil on the stove.

ANCHOVY PASTE

You may find anchovy paste, which comes in tubes, more convenient to use and milder-tasting than fillets. Note, however, that the paste contains more than anchovies. Additions may include oil, vinegar, water and spices. About ½ tsp (2 mL) anchovy paste is the equivalent of one anchovy fillet. Keep anchovy paste in the fridge for up to a month after it has been opened.

CRAB

There are more than 4,000 varieties of sea and freshwater crabs. The most commonly consumed are North America's blue crabs and Asia's blue swimmer crabs. It takes 10 to 15 crabs to extract 1½ pounds (750 g) of meat. No wonder crabmeat is expensive!

TYPES OF CANNED CRAB

Crab may be shelf-stable or pasteurized, packed in cans or tubs. Pasteurized crab must be refrigerated. It has a shelf life of about 18 months. Once opened, handle it like fresh seafood: keep it in the fridge, securely packaged, and consume it within two days. Although generally more expensive, pasteurized crab is preferable. Shelf-stable crab is heated to a higher temperature for a longer time than pasteurized crab, and this can take a toll on the delicate meat. However, shelf-stable crab is fine in dips and some salads, sandwiches, soups and pastas when you want to enjoy crab more economically.

GRADES OF CRABMEAT

Crabmeat is graded by the size of the pieces. There is also a differentiation between meat from the body and from the claws. Designations vary by brand.

In crabspeak, the chunks are called lumps. White meat is from the body, or carapace. Claw meat is pink-brown and comes from the pincers, swimming fins and legs. Which tastes best is up to the taster. Some people prefer the milder white lump crabmeat, others the "crabbier" claw meat. Pricewise, white and lump trump brown and flaked.

The largest lump white meat comes from the muscles that power the swimming fins. There are only two per crab, and the bigger the crab, the bigger the lumps. This top grade is given appetizing names such as "colossal," "imperial" and "jumbo." A step down are varieties such as "super lump" (broken jumbo lumps and large pieces of body meat), "special" (small pieces from the body) and "backfin" (large and small pieces).

Large lump crabmeat is best for salads, or for when the boss is coming for dinner. Versatile special and backfin grades work in dishes ranging from soup to casseroles. Flaked crabmeat is okay in some dips and sandwich spreads, but be careful with it — enthusiastic mixing can turn it into a paste. Use claw meat for recipes in which you want the most crab flavor. It's also good for finer-textured, easier-to-work-with crab cakes.

The designations on shelf-stable cans include lump, chunk, white meat, flake (white), claw, leg and pink (claw and white meat). Cans labeled "15% leg meat" include mainly fine shreds with small whole leg chunks (do not confuse this with the heartier "claw meat"). Flake or "salad" crab is least expensive; some is so fine it appears minced. In spite of its name, salad crab is too fine for green salads, but it can be mixed with mayonnaise in spreads and dips.

Crabmeat should be moist and springy and smell of briny seawater, not ammonia — a sign of spoilage. Lump crabmeat should be creamy white (no grays, blues or greens, please). Check labels for best-before dates. Don't keep leftovers sitting around while you wait for culinary inspiration. Freezing is possible but not recommended. If you must freeze crabmeat, it's best to first add the crab to a prepared dish.

CLAMS

Clams are the most popular of the canned bivalves, for good reason. They cut down the work and expense involved in cooking iconic dishes that range from clam chowder to clam pie to spaghetti with clams.

There are more than 2,000 varieties of clams, from hard-shell to soft-shell and from saltwater to freshwater. These days clams are mostly farmed, but you can find wild clams in a can too. East Coast hard-shells are called quahogs and are categorized according to size: button, littleneck, topneck, cherrystone and chowder. They live in deeper water. West Coast hard-shells include Pacific littlenecks, pismos and butter clams. Soft-shell clams live in tidal areas. Their shells are not actually soft but rather thin and brittle. They don't close fully because their siphons protrude. Soft-shell clams include steamers, razor clams and the comical-looking geoduck, with its huge siphon.

CLAM JUICE

Another handy pantry item is shelf-stable bottled clam juice, which is sold in most supermarkets. If you don't have fish stock you can substitute equal portions of clam juice and water or stock. Do not use the liquid from a can of clams, because it is likely to contain additives such as preservatives.

TYPES OF CANNED CLAMS

Clams that are commonly sold canned range from those ubiquitous baby clams to their meatier cousins. The baby clams, including yellow clams and tiny manilas, are so delicate they can get lost in casseroles or hearty noodle dishes. However, they are fine in some dips, soups and pastas. Baby clams are commonly packed in water in cans or jars. You may also find them smoked and packed in oil.

For most dishes I prefer the larger, meatier canned clams, particularly surf clams. Depending on one's point of view, they are either pleasantly chewy or tough. Personally, I appreciate that they give you something to sink your teeth into. They look better and taste substantial in chowders and on pizza. Some are canned whole, some chopped. Availability and types vary from area to area. Big surf clams (also known as sea, hen or bar clams or skimmers) and pink clams (also known as machas) are mild and sweet. Ocean clams (also known as quahogs) are darker and more pungent.

MACKEREL

Some of the recipe variations in this book suggest mackerel as a substitution. Mackerel may be popular in countries as far-flung as Britain and Japan, but it gets little respect in North America. Some people complain it is too "fishy," but I find it surprisingly tasty. The oily, flaky, dark, soft flesh is packed in water, brine or olive or other kinds of oil. Large segments are stuffed into full-sized cans, while small tins hold fillets or sardine-like pieces.

Further Adventures in Seafood

Even more kinds of canned fish and seafood are available for you to discover if you are feeling adventurous, or if you need a shelf-stable option when fresh is not available for a favorite recipe, such as Lobster Thermidor. The following choices can be substituted for the key ingredients in some of the recipes in this book.

If you ever come across something called **kippers** on a menu (a popular breakfast item in the United Kingdom), know that kipper is not the name of the fish. It is a way of preparing a fish, usually a herring, by lightly salting, splitting in half and cold smoking. Kippers are available tinned.

Looking for a different treat for your tongue and tastebuds? Try **roe**, or fish eggs, which can mean anything from haute cuisine's beluga caviar to that jar of lumpfish roe you pick up in the supermarket.

Although most people buy fresh or frozen **shrimp** nowadays, shrimp is also available in convenient shelf-stable cans.

Lobster canning was big business a century ago, but now that fresh and frozen lobster is easier to transport, you'll have to search hard to find any canned lobster in the supermarket.

Tinned **oysters** have little in common with fresh oysters in terms of taste and texture, but they are delicious in their own right, especially when smoked and packed in oil. In North America, smoked oysters caught on only after the Second World War. They were popularized by smart 1960s hostesses, no doubt sporting beehives and stilettos as they passed them around as hors d'oeuvres.

Canned **mussels**, available smoked or plain, have a lower profile than tinned oysters but are well worth a try.

Canned **squid**, packed in its own ink and brine, surely tastes better when labeled "calamari," its Italian name. Canned chunks are better than whole baby squid, which tend to be rubbery.

Octopus, however, is surprisingly tasty from the can — if you like octopus to begin with. I have used canned octopus on pizza and it can be substituted for other canned seafood in some salads and pastas.

CANNED SEAFOOD FAQ

IS THAT A TIN OR A CAN OR A TIN CAN?

Cans were originally called tins because the metal was tin-plated. Although "tin" is more of a Britishism, nowadays folks use "tinned" and "canned" interchangeably. I think of the puck-shaped containers as cans and the oval containers as tins, but you can call them whatever you wish. Manufacturers play with sizes and variations in containers, although they all serve the same function: to preserve food. Some "canned" seafood, such as imported tuna, comes in a jar. Some, such as crabmeat, comes in a plastic tub with a metal lid. The latest thing is the metal-and-plastic pouch.

WHAT IS CANNING?

All food contains bacteria, which, over time, will cause it to spoil. One way to prevent spoilage is to seal food in a sterile, airtight container and subject it to enough heat to destroy microorganisms. This canning process cooks the food and changes the taste and texture.

Canned seafood may be shelf-stable or pasteurized. Shelf-stable seafood is sterilized using high heat. It can be stored at room temperature. Pasteurized seafood is heated to lower temperatures for shorter periods of time. This reduces the number of harmful microorganisms but doesn't inactivate them all. The food lasts way longer than it would au naturel, but it must be refrigerated to increase its shelf life (the same as with pasteurized milk). Pasteurization is usually reserved for higher-end products such as crabmeat.

STORING CANNED FISH

Nothing lasts forever — even in a can. Canning generally gives seafood a shelf life of about two years, depending on how it is stored. Check best-before dates on all canned seafood before purchasing and using it.

Keep shelf-stable cans in a cool, dry spot where the temperature doesn't fluctuate. If a can bulges or leaks or the seams look damaged, throw it out. Keep pasteurized seafood in the fridge. If you are not sure whether a can should be refrigerated, take your cue from the supermarket as well as reading the label. Do not put unopened cans or pouches in the freezer. Freezing can weaken the seams or even burst the container.

After opening a can, use the product immediately or transfer it to a storage tub with a tight lid and refrigerate. Depending on the seafood, leftovers can be kept for one to three days. I don't recommend freezing leftovers as a habit, as that may create an unpleasant texture.

GREENER LABELS

Consumers drive change with their wallets. The dizzying array of canned seafood choices is expanding as manufacturers respond to the demands of environmentally concerned and health-conscious shoppers who want to know what they are eating. Vague labels are being replaced with more informative ones, and green brands are the latest thing. Some labels tell you what species you are eating and where and how it was caught. Premium boutique brands boast that they can track their fish from boat to can, identifying the vessel, captain, flag, harvest method, area of capture and trip dates.

Aquaculture is another loaded topic, with too many pros and cons to debate here. If you are concerned about farmed seafood, look for the word "wild" on the label. There are plenty of greener choices in terms of canned seafood. For a full overview, check any of the sea-watch organizations online. Examples include SeaChoice (www.seachoice.org) and Seafood Watch (www.seafoodwatch.org).

HEALTHY OPTIONS

Seafood is lower in calories and saturated fat than meat. It is rich in omega-3 fatty acids (the so-called heart-healthy fish oils) and the edible soft bones in some fish are a good source of calcium. Fatty coldwater fish — such as salmon, tuna, anchovies, herring, sardines and mackerel — are top sources of omega-3 fats.

Unfortunately, mercury levels in some seafood, both fresh and canned, is a concern. In fact, women of childbearing age and young children have been advised to minimize their intake of fish that are high in mercury.

Virtually all fish contain traces of mercury, but most do not contain amounts that are potentially harmful to your health. Contaminants such as mercury concentrate in fatty tissues such as belly flesh, skin and dark meat.

Fish are what they eat. Big predatory carnivores contain the most methylmercury, as the toxin is technically known. The larger, older and higher up in the food chain a fish is, the more contaminants it carries from years of gobbling up little fish. This means that smaller fish, such as skipjack, contain less mercury than larger ones, such as albacore tuna, and the little sardine and short-lived salmon will contain less mercury than a giant bluefin tuna.

The bottom line: most experts say that the benefits of eating fish outweigh the risks, as long as you do not over-consume seafood that is high in contaminants.

WATER VERSUS OIL

Should you choose seafood packed in water or in oil? It depends on your recipe. Are you going to add sauce or mayonnaise? Are you going to drain the oil anyway? Then choose water-packed seafood or the "no-drain" type. However, be aware that fish packed in oil is superior because it has a silkier texture and richer flavor. Choose fish packed in oil if you are planning to use the oil or are willing to spend the calories. Oil-packed tuna, for instance, has 25 to 50 percent more calories compared to the water-packed kind.

Extra virgin olive oil is the best of the available options. Strangely, anchovies and sardines are commonly packed in extra virgin olive oil, but not most tuna. It is usually packed in mere olive oil, a lower grade that includes refined oil stripped of antioxidants and flavor.

When fish is packed in olive oil, I recommend that you drain the oil from the can and use it in your recipe. For one thing, you've paid for it. For another, omega-3 fats leach from the fish into the oil, which is not the case with fish packed in water. Definitely don't discard the savory, salty oil from anchovies. In addition, oils from smoked fish, oysters or mussels are particularly tasty, even though they may be vegetable or seed oils.

I wonder about the worth of paying more for fish canned in refined soybean, seed or vegetable oils. The same goes for seafood packed in broth or broth and oil. Depending on which company is talking, the broth may add flavor or make the fish taste milder.

WHAT ABOUT THE BONES?

Some canned fish — including salmon, sardines, mackerel and anchovies — contain small bones. Heat processing makes those bones soft, feathery and edible. I recommend that you eat the bones for the calcium they contain. I eat the tiny bones in salmon but usually pull out the backbone. The same goes for the skin, which is rich in omega-3 fats. If you don't like the skin or bones or if you want a smoother texture in your recipe (a dip, for example), discard them, or buy boneless, skinless fish.

Occasionally consumers find stray bones in tuna. These are not edible — discard them. Also, beware of shell fragments in canned crab and other shellfish. The cannery tries to remove them all, but some do slip past inspection.

AFTER OPENING THE CAN

Gently drain and rinse canned fish and seafood with cold water whenever practical. This sloughs off some of the sodium and unwanted preservatives. It also refreshes the product, which can start to taste tinny in its liquid. This is not recommended for crab but I do it anyway, except when it comes in tiny flakes. I may rinse solid tuna, but not salmon — it gets too waterlogged. Do not, of course, rinse seafood, plain or smoked, that is packed in oil.

Don't be afraid to gently squeeze seafood to remove excess moisture. This isn't necessary when you are adding seafood to a sauce, but it is probably crucial if you're making fish burgers or a pie. Whether you rinse it or not, canned crab may seem soggy because the meat is porous. Brief poaching in butter or oil, as part of the recipe, evaporates excess moisture and tenderizes the meat.

WATCH THE SALT

Be careful with the salt shaker, especially if you are adding seafood at the end of a recipe. Seafood is salted during canning — far too much, in my opinion. Choose seafood labeled "low-sodium" or check the labels and compare among brands.

I normally use coarse sea salt in seafood dishes, but I switched to table salt when testing the recipes for this book because it is standardized and more commonly used. If you want to substitute coarse sea salt or kosher salt, increase the quantities called for by a third to a half, or go by taste.

WORKING WITH CAN SIZES

When developing the recipes in this book, I gave priority to using one or two cans per dish and stuck to sizes that are commonly available in supermarkets. However, there are regional differences, as well as odd sizes caused by disparities between metric and imperial measures. Also, some products are standardized while others come in a variety of sizes.

Luckily, most canned seafood recipes are very forgiving. Just pick a size or weight that's close to the one in the ingredient list. (Note that some seafood labels state both net and drained weights. The latter is more accurate.) Dips, soups, pastas and the like should give you no problems. However, stick closely to the can size in the few cases where the amount used is crucial to the texture, such as crab cakes and fishballs.

Getting Started

Tuna Tapenade	32
Hot Crab Dip	33
Bagna Cauda Dip	34
Clam, Bacon and Chive Dip	35
Catalan Clams and Ham	36
Deviled Eggs with Tuna	37
Salmon, Spinach and Sweet Potato Frittata	38
Curried Scrambled Eggs and Crab	39
Salmon and Egg Smørrebrød	41
Sardines with Roast Spuds, Smoked Paprika Oil and Lemon	42
Crab and Corn Griddle Cakes	43

TUNA TAPENADE

> **MAKES ABOUT 1½ CUPS (375 ML) — 6 APPETIZER SERVINGS** •
> Tapenade is a versatile olive and anchovy paste from Provence. Adding tuna transforms it from a condiment to a spread. Whet your appetite by slathering it on crackers or crostini, liven up hard-cooked eggs by serving tapenade alongside, or dollop it on cheese pizza just before serving.

Food processor

2 cloves garlic

1 cup (250 mL) pitted black olives (see Tip, below)

1 cup (250 mL) basil leaves (¼ oz/7 g)

3 anchovy fillets

1 tbsp (15 mL) capers, rinsed and drained

2 tbsp (30 mL) extra virgin olive oil

2 cans (each 3 oz/85 g) tuna in olive oil, with oil

1 tsp (5 mL) freshly squeezed lemon juice, optional

Freshly ground black pepper

1 In food processor fitted with the metal blade, with motor running, drop garlic through the feed tube to chop. Add olives, basil, anchovies and capers and process until puréed. Scrape down the sides of the bowl. With the motor running, drizzle olive oil through the feed tube and process until incorporated.

2 Transfer to a serving bowl. Add tuna with its oil and, using a fork, break into flakes and mix in well. Add lemon juice, if using, and season to taste with pepper.

TIP

Niçoise olives are traditionally used in tapenade, but other black olives work well too.

VARIATIONS

Mix tapenade with hot pasta and serve as a main. Added to room-temperature pasta, it makes a salad.

To create a dip, stir tapenade to taste into 1 cup (250 mL) soft cream cheese.

Smooth out tapenade with mayonnaise, spoon it over a lettuce leaf and serve it with crusty bread alongside.

Substitute an equal quantity of salmon, mackerel or sardines for the tuna.

HOT CRAB DIP

MAKES ABOUT 1 CUP (250 ML) — 4 APPETIZER SERVINGS • Hot crab dip is usually baked, but you can make batches in the microwave. I recommend microwaving smaller batches for almost instant gratification. After all, how much hot crab dip can you consume before it gets cold?

4 oz (125 g) block cream cheese, softened	1 green onion (white and light green parts), minced
3 tbsp (45 mL) shredded Cheddar cheese	1 tbsp (15 mL) minced red bell pepper
1 tbsp (15 mL) mayonnaise	1 can (4.25 oz/120 g) crabmeat, rinsed and drained (see Tips, below)
1 to 2 tsp (5 to 10 mL) freshly squeezed lime juice, divided	
½ tsp (2 mL) Worcestershire sauce	Salt and freshly ground white pepper
½ tsp (2 mL) hot pepper sauce	Sweet paprika

1 In a microwave-safe bowl, using a fork, mash together cream cheese, Cheddar, mayonnaise, 1 tsp (5 mL) lime juice, Worcestershire sauce, hot pepper sauce, onion and red pepper. Gently squeeze the crab to remove excess moisture and add to the bowl. Fold in gently and season to taste with salt and pepper. Add remaining 1 tsp (5 mL) lime juice if you prefer a tangier dip.

2 Microwave on High for 1 to 2 minutes, until dip is bubbly at the edges. Stir well and return to microwave for 30 to 60 seconds, until hot and bubbly.

3 Scrape dip into a small serving bowl and sprinkle paprika generously over top. Serve immediately.

TIPS

You can prepare the dip a day ahead, but be savvy about food safety.

It's okay to use less expensive flaked crab in this recipe.

VARIATION

If you want to double or triple the recipe, it is best to bake the dip. After completing Step 1, scrape mixture into an ovenproof dish. Bake in a 375°F (190°C) oven until heated through and bubbly at the edges. Stir and sprinkle paprika overtop. Baking time depends on amount and dish size. A triple batch baked in a 4-cup (1 L) casserole takes about 30 minutes.

Experiment with other seafood such as tuna, salmon, mackerel, clams, oysters or mussels.

BAGNA CAUDA DIP

> **MAKES ABOUT ¾ CUP (175 ML)** • Anchovies, garlic and oil are transformed into something marvelous in Piedmont, Italy, the home of bagna cauda. This mouthwatering partner for crusty bread and steamed or raw vegetables is a cross between a fondue and a dip. The name translates as "hot bath." Bagna cauda is decadently drippy, so it's easy to see why personal dipping plates have replaced communal pots. Compatible veggies include baby squash and zucchini, artichoke hearts, cauliflower florets, grape tomatoes and green beans.

1 tin (2 oz/50 g) anchovies in extra virgin olive oil, drained (oil reserved)	4 large cloves garlic, minced
½ cup (125 mL) extra virgin olive oil (approx.)	3 tbsp (45 mL) unsalted butter (see Tips, below)
	Freshly ground black pepper

1 Soak anchovies for 10 minutes in a small bowl of cold water. Drain and pat dry, then chop coarsely. Transfer to a very small skillet or saucepan.

2 Pour reserved oil from the anchovies into a measuring cup and add enough extra virgin olive oil to equal ½ cup (125 mL). Add to anchovies and bring to a simmer over medium heat. Reduce heat to low and simmer for 5 minutes, until anchovies start to dissolve. Using a small, heatproof spatula, mash anchovies against the bottom of the pan. Stir in garlic. Cook for 1 minute, until garlic softens.

3 Remove from heat. Stir in butter until melted and blended. Season to taste with pepper. Serve warm, in individual dipping bowls.

TIPS

It is important to mince the garlic as finely as possible. Better still, push it through a press.

Using unsalted butter is particularly important in recipes featuring anchovies, which are salty enough on their own.

In addition, the amount of salt in salted butter varies by brand, and it contains more moisture, which may affect some recipes. Salt also masks rancidity, which means you can be more confident that you're using a fresh product when your butter isn't salted.

VARIATION

Try using Bagna Cauda instead of oil or butter when making scrambled eggs. Yum!

CLAM, BACON AND CHIVE DIP

MAKES ABOUT 2 CUPS (500 ML) — 8 APPETIZER SERVINGS • Clams and bacon go so well together. The clam juice punches up the flavor of this dip, which is delicious with toasted pitas or crackers.

4 slices bacon, coarsely chopped

8 oz (250 g) soft cream cheese (1 cup/250 mL)

1 tbsp (15 mL) bottled clam juice

1 to 2 tsp (5 to 10 mL) freshly squeezed lime juice

1 tsp (5 mL) Worcestershire sauce

1 can (5 oz/142 g) baby clams, rinsed, drained and chopped

¼ cup (60 mL) chopped chives

2 tbsp (30 mL) finely chopped red bell pepper

2 to 4 tbsp (30 to 60 mL) sour cream

Salt and freshly ground white pepper

1 In a skillet, over medium heat, cook bacon, stirring often, for 5 minutes, until browned and crisp. Using a slotted spoon, transfer it to a plate lined with paper towels to drain.

2 In a bowl, using a fork, mix cream cheese, clam juice, 1 tsp (5 mL) lime juice and Worcestershire sauce until blended. Stir in clams, chives, red pepper and just enough sour cream to reach dipping consistency. Season to taste with salt and pepper.

3 Crumble in the bacon and stir. Add remaining 1 tsp (5 mL) lime juice, if desired, to adjust the tartness. Taste and adjust salt, if necessary. Serve immediately.

TIPS

You can use lower-fat cream cheese and sour cream.

For convenience, make this dip up to 1 day ahead. Complete Steps 1 and 2 and cover and refrigerate the bacon and clam mixtures separately. When ready to serve, complete Step 3.

Substitute an equal quantity of salmon or crab for the clams.

GETTING STARTED

CATALAN CLAMS AND HAM

MAKES 2 TO 4 APPETIZER SERVINGS • Small plates are tasty options on modern menus. Canned clams are the shortcut to enjoying this savory Spanish tapas dish. Mop up the sauce with crusty bread.

¼ cup (60 mL) extra virgin olive oil	½ cup (125 mL) dry white wine
2 large cloves garlic, minced	2 tbsp (30 mL) chopped cilantro leaves
1 can (5 oz/142 g) surf or meaty clams, rinsed, drained and coarsely chopped	⅛ tsp (0.5 mL) freshly ground black pepper
2 oz (60 g) sliced Serrano ham, cut in thin strips	¼ tsp (1 mL) smoked sweet paprika

1 In a skillet, heat oil over medium-high heat until shimmery. Remove from heat and stir in garlic for 30 seconds. Return to element and add clams and ham. Cook, stirring often, for 1 minute. Add wine, cilantro and freshly ground pepper. Cook, stirring often, for 2 to 3 minutes, until reduced and slightly thickened.

2 Just before serving, sprinkle paprika over top.

TIP
You won't need salt because the ham and clams are already salty.

VARIATION
If you don't have Serrano ham, substitute prosciutto. Both are cured meats and sliced ultra-thin.

DEVILED EGGS WITH TUNA

MAKES 24 • You can embellish deviled eggs with all kinds of seafood, herbs and spices. Here's one idea to get you started.

12 large eggs

1 can (3 oz/85 g) tuna in olive oil, with oil

¼ cup (60 mL) mayonnaise

1 tsp (5 mL) freshly squeezed lemon juice

1 tsp (5 mL) honey mustard

1 tsp (5 mL) capers, rinsed, drained, patted dry and chopped

Salt and freshly ground black pepper

1 Place eggs in a pan and add enough water to cover by about ½ inch (1 cm). Bring to a boil over high heat. Immediately cover pan and turn off heat. Set aside for 10 minutes.

2 Run eggs under cold running water. Crack and peel off shells. Using a wet knife, cut each egg in half lengthwise.

3 Using a small spoon, scoop out yolks and transfer to a bowl. Add tuna, with oil, mayonnaise, lemon juice, mustard and capers. Mash with a fork. Season to taste with salt.

4 Pipe or spoon mixture into cavities of egg whites (see Tips, below). Grind pepper over top to taste.

TIPS

Extremists press the yolks through a sieve for a smoother filling. Don't bother — you will just drive yourself crazy.

You can use a food processor fitted with the metal blade to mix the filling.

If you don't have a piping bag, use a zip-lock bag with a little hole cut in one corner.

To keep deviled eggs from sliding around on the serving plate, line it with a doily or paper towel. You can cut a thin slice off the base of each egg, but it will look strange. If you make these a lot, spring for a deviled egg platter and/or storage tub.

Try mashing the yolks with smoked oysters or mussels. You can also use salmon, anchovies or crab in the filling.

SALMON, SPINACH AND SWEET POTATO FRITTATA

MAKES 4 TO 6 SERVINGS • A frittata is an easy choice for brunch or a family dinner. It's basically an open-faced omelet, so you don't have to fuss with folding, flipping or rolling. It's finished under the broiler — the heat causes the eggs to puff attractively.

1 small sweet potato (about 8 oz/250 g), peeled and cut in ¼-inch (0.5 cm) dice	1 tbsp (15 mL) extra virgin olive oil
1½ cups (375 mL) stemmed, torn spinach leaves (1 oz/30 g)	1 onion, diced
8 large eggs	1 small green bell pepper, cut in tiny dice
¾ tsp (3 mL) salt	1 clove garlic, minced
⅛ tsp (0.5 mL) freshly ground black pepper	1 can (6 oz/170 g) boneless, skinless salmon, drained

Preheat broiler, placing oven rack one level down from top position

1 In a pot of boiling salted water over medium heat, cook sweet potato for 3 to 4 minutes, until tender but firm. Using a mesh scoop, transfer to a sieve. Drain and set aside.

2 Return water to a boil. Add spinach and blanch for 30 seconds. Drain. When cool enough to handle, squeeze dry and chop coarsely. Set aside.

3 In a bowl, whisk together eggs, salt and pepper.

4 In a 12-inch (30 cm) cast-iron skillet (see Tip, below), heat oil over medium-high heat until shimmery. Add onion, green pepper and garlic and cook, stirring often, for about 5 minutes, until vegetables soften. Add spinach and sweet potato and cook, stirring, for 1 minute. Add eggs and stir gently to distribute ingredients. Squeeze salmon to remove excess moisture and scatter it over the eggs. Cook for about 2 minutes, occasionally lifting edges and tilting pan to let uncooked egg run underneath, until bottom has set and browned but top is a bit runny.

5 Place skillet under preheated broiler for 1 to 2 minutes to set top. Serve immediately.

TIP

If you don't have a cast-iron skillet, use a nonstick skillet and wrap the handle in foil to protect it from the heat of the broiler.

CURRIED SCRAMBLED EGGS AND CRAB

MAKES 4 SERVINGS • No more ho-hum scrambled eggs, please. Try this delicious melange instead.

8 large eggs

¼ tsp (1 mL) salt (approx.)

⅛ tsp (0.5 mL) freshly ground black pepper

1 tbsp (15 mL) oil

2 large green onions (white and light green parts), cut diagonally into ½-inch (1 cm) segments

1 jalapeño pepper, seeded and cut in ⅛-inch (3 mm) dice

2 tsp (10 mL) curry powder (see Tips, below)

1 plum tomato, cut in ¼-inch (0.5 cm) dice

¼ cup (60 mL) chopped cilantro leaves, divided

1 can (4.25 oz/120 g) crabmeat, rinsed and drained (see Tips, below)

Cayenne pepper

1 In a bowl, lightly whisk eggs, ¼ tsp (1 mL) salt and pepper.

2 In a nonstick skillet, heat oil over medium-high heat until shimmery. Add green onions and jalapeño and cook, stirring often, for 2 to 3 minutes, until they turn golden. Stir in curry powder. Add tomato and 3 tbsp (45 mL) cilantro. Cook for 1 minute, stirring constantly, until liquid evaporates.

3 Reduce heat to medium-low. Add eggs and cook, stirring occasionally, for 2 minutes, until they start to set but are still slightly moist. Fold in crab. Cook, stirring occasionally, for 1 minute, until eggs are just set. Add salt to taste, if necessary.

4 Sprinkle cayenne and remaining 1 tbsp (15 mL) cilantro over top. Serve immediately.

TIPS

Use good-quality curry powder. The "brand X" ones contain too much turmeric, which gives them a bitter edge.

You can dress this dish up or down. Use either pasteurized lump/claw crabmeat or shelf-stable small-chunk/leg crabmeat.

Substitute an equal quantity of tuna, salmon, mackerel or mussels for the crab.

SALMON AND EGG SMØRREBRØD

MAKES 4 SERVINGS • Danish open-faced sandwiches on dark rye are eaten with a knife and fork. In this delicious translation, canned salmon replaces the traditional (and pricier) smoked salmon.

4 oz (125 g) block cream cheese, softened (½ cup/125 mL)	4 slices dark rye
1 can (7½ oz/213 g) salmon, drained, deboned and broken into flakes	20 thin slices peeled English cucumber (about ½ cup/125 mL), patted dry
4 large eggs	¼ cup (60 mL) chopped red bell pepper
Salt and freshly ground black pepper	4 tsp (20 mL) capers, rinsed, drained and chopped (see Tip, below)
1 tbsp (15 mL) unsalted butter	

1. In a bowl, using a fork, mix together cream cheese and salmon.

2. In a small bowl, whisk together eggs, and salt and pepper to taste.

3. In a 10-inch (25 cm) nonstick skillet, melt butter over medium heat. Add eggs and cook for about 2 minutes, until firm, stirring at first to incorporate uncooked egg, then leaving the mixture to set. Remove from heat.

4. Spread salmon mixture over bread, dividing equally. Transfer to individual serving plates. Arrange cucumber slices over top, dividing equally. Divide eggs into 4 portions and arrange on top. Sprinkle red pepper and capers evenly over eggs. Serve immediately.

TIP

Capers come bottled in brine or dry-salted. The latter are less common but superior in pungency and firmness. You can use either type in this recipe.

Substitute canned smoked salmon or tuna or smoked oysters or mussels. You can also try mackerel.

SARDINES WITH ROAST SPUDS, SMOKED PAPRIKA OIL AND LEMON

MAKES 2 TO 4 SERVINGS • This simple meal of sardines, greens and potatoes is exceptionally tasty.

Rimmed baking sheet

¼ cup (60 mL) extra virgin olive oil

1 tsp (5 mL) smoked sweet paprika

1 tbsp + 1 tsp (20 mL) finely grated lemon zest, divided

½ tsp (2 mL) salt (approx.)

⅛ tsp (0.5 mL) freshly ground black pepper

1 lb (500 g) mini potatoes (about 1½ inches/4 cm in diameter), scrubbed and halved (see Tips, below)

4 cups (1 L) baby arugula leaves (about 2 oz/60 g)

1 tin (3.75 oz/106 g) sardines, drained

4 lemon wedges

Preheat oven to 400°F (200°C)

1 In a measuring cup, whisk together oil, paprika, 1 tbsp (15 mL) lemon zest, salt and pepper.

2 In a bowl, toss potatoes with 2 tbsp (30 mL) of the oil mixture. Arrange, cut side up, on baking sheet and roast in preheated oven for 40 to 45 minutes, until tender and golden. Transfer to a bowl and toss gently with 1 tbsp (15 mL) of remaining oil mixture. Set aside to cool for 10 to 15 minutes (you don't want to make the arugula limp).

3 Line a small platter with arugula. Place potatoes on top and arrange sardines alongside. Drizzle remaining oil mixture over sardines. Sprinkle salt, to taste, over top. Scatter remaining 1 tsp (5 mL) lemon zest over potatoes. Place lemon wedges alongside to squeeze liberally over sardines and potatoes. Serve immediately.

TIP

Sardines break easily. For the best presentation, handle them gently to keep them intact.

Substitute an equal quantity of tuna, salmon or mackerel for the sardines.

CRAB AND CORN GRIDDLE CAKES

MAKES ABOUT 22 GRIDDLE CAKES — 8 TO 10 SERVINGS • These delicious morsels start as polenta and morph into griddle cakes. They seem to get snapped up the second they leave the griddle.

Nonstick griddle

2 cups (500 mL) all-purpose flour
1 tsp (5 mL) salt
1 tsp (5 mL) baking powder
½ tsp (2 mL) baking soda
1½ cups (375 mL) buttermilk
1 large egg
2 tbsp (30 mL) extra virgin olive oil, divided
1½ cups (375 mL) water
½ cup (125 mL) fine cornmeal
1¼ cups (300 mL) canned crabmeat (6 oz/175 g), rinsed and drained (see Tip, below)
1 cup (250 mL) corn kernels, patted dry
¼ cup (60 mL) chopped basil
Lumpfish caviar (roe), rinsed and drained, optional

1. Sift flour, salt, baking powder and baking soda into a bowl.

2. In a large measuring cup, lightly whisk together buttermilk, egg and 1 tbsp (15 mL) oil.

3. In a small saucepan, whisk together water and cornmeal. Bring to a simmer over high heat, whisking often. Reduce heat to medium-low and simmer for 5 minutes, whisking often.

4. Scrape cornmeal mixture into a large bowl. Whisking constantly, add buttermilk mixture. Stir in flour mixture just until moistened (do not overmix). Gently squeeze crab to remove excess moisture. Add to bowl with corn and basil.

5. Heat griddle over medium heat. Before cooking each batch, brush griddle lightly with some of the remaining oil. Ladle ¼ cup (60 mL) batter per cake onto hot griddle. Cook for about 2 minutes, until bubbles form on the tops and bottoms are golden. Flip and cook for 1 to 2 minutes more, until bottoms are golden and cakes are cooked through. Keep warm and continue with remaining batter.

6. Before serving, sprinkle caviar, if using, over each griddle cake.

TIP
Use small lump or claw crabmeat instead of the flaked kind.

Substitute an equal quantity of salmon or mackerel for the crab. You can also substitute baby clams.

GETTING STARTED

Soups

Salmon and White Bean Soup with Oniony Croutons	46
Salmon and Roasted Garlic Bisque with Cajun Croutons	48
Salmon, Corn and Herb Chowder with Pepper Jack	50
Clams in Herb Broth with Angel Hair Pasta	51
New England Clam Chowder	52
Manhattan Clam Chowder	53
Faux Pho	54
Soba Noodles with Fishballs and Snow Peas	56
Crab, Watercress and Egg Drop Soup	58
Thai Coconut Crab Soup	59
Creamy Crab and Poblano Soup	60

SALMON AND WHITE BEAN SOUP WITH ONIONY CROUTONS

MAKES ABOUT 7 CUPS (1.75 L) — 4 TO 6 SERVINGS • You can easily make a meal of this filling soup. It provides both nourishment and satisfaction.

Rimmed baking sheet
Blender or food processor

CROUTONS

2 tbsp (30 mL) extra virgin olive oil
2 tsp (10 mL) onion powder
½ tsp (2 mL) dried parsley
½ tsp (2 mL) salt
⅛ tsp (0.5 mL) freshly ground black pepper
3 cups (750 mL) diced (½ inch/1 cm) crusty bread

SOUP

2 tbsp (30 mL) extra virgin olive oil
1 onion, diced
1 carrot, coarsely chopped
1 stalk celery, diced
2 cloves garlic, chopped
2 cups (500 mL) chicken or vegetable stock
2 cups (500 mL) water
2 cans (each 14 to 19 oz/398 to 540 mL) cannellini (white kidney) beans, drained and rinsed (see Tips, page 47)
2 tbsp (30 mL) chopped sage leaves, divided
1 can (7½ oz/213 g) salmon, drained, deboned and broken into small chunks
Salt and freshly ground black pepper

Preheat oven to 400°F (200°C)

1 CROUTONS: In a large bowl, stir together oil, onion powder, parsley, salt and pepper. Add bread cubes and toss until well coated. Spread evenly on baking sheet and bake in preheated oven for 8 to 10 minutes, shaking once or twice, until golden brown and crispy.

2 SOUP: In a large saucepan, heat oil over medium heat until shimmery. Add onion, carrot, celery and garlic. Cook, stirring, for about 5 minutes, until vegetables soften and turn golden. Add stock, water, beans and half the sage. Bring the mixture to a simmer over medium-high heat. Reduce heat to low and simmer for 30 minutes, until vegetables are very soft.

3 Ladle out 2 cups (500 mL) of soup and set aside. In batches, transfer remainder to blender or food processor fitted with the metal blade (or use an immersion blender) and purée. Return to saucepan, if necessary. Add reserved soup and salmon and season to taste with salt and pepper. Bring to a simmer over medium heat and cook until heated through.

4 Ladle into warm bowls and scatter croutons over top, dividing equally. Garnish with remaining sage and serve immediately.

TIPS

Because the croutons are baked, they will get soggier faster than fried ones.

I use 19-ounce (540 mL) cans of beans. If you use a smaller size, the soup will be thinner. You can compensate by starting with 1½ cups (375 mL) water and adding more at the end if desired.

Use milder-tasting pink salmon in this dish.

Substitute tuna or mackerel for the salmon.

SALMON AND ROASTED GARLIC BISQUE WITH CAJUN CROUTONS

MAKES ABOUT 4 CUPS (1 L) — 4 SMALL SERVINGS • Vampires need not apply for a bowl of this garlicky soup, which strikes a delicious balance between pungent and mellow. Almost any canned fish will work with the creamy base and crispy garnish.

Rimmed baking sheet

Blender or food processor

CROUTONS

1 tbsp (15 mL) Cajun seasoning (see Tips, page 49)

1 tsp (5 mL) garlic powder

2 tbsp (30 mL) extra virgin olive oil

1 small loaf ciabatta (about 6 oz/175 g) or demi-baguette, cut in ½-inch (1 cm) dice

SOUP

2 heads garlic

⅛ tsp (0.5 mL) vegetable or olive oil

2 tbsp (30 mL) unsalted butter

1 onion, diced

1 potato (about 8 oz/250 g), diced (see Tips, page 49)

1 bay leaf

1 tsp (5 mL) thyme leaves

3 cups (750 mL) chicken or vegetable stock

½ cup (125 mL) half-and-half (10%) cream

1 can (7½ oz/213 g) salmon, drained, deboned and broken into chunks

Salt and freshly ground black pepper

Preheat oven to 400°F (200°C)

1 CROUTONS: In a small bowl, stir together Cajun seasoning and garlic powder. Set aside.

2 In a large skillet, heat oil over medium-high heat until shimmery. Stir in bread and cook, occasionally flipping with a spatula, for about 5 minutes, until golden brown. Remove from heat. Sprinkle reserved spice mixture evenly over top and toss thoroughly. Transfer to baking sheet and spread evenly. Set aside to cool.

3 SOUP: Meanwhile, remove any loose papery skin from the garlic heads. Cut a thin slice off the top of each head. Place each head on a square of foil and drizzle oil over top. Wrap in foil and roast in preheated oven for about 45 minutes, until tender. Remove from oven and set aside to cool. Press roasted garlic cloves out of their skins and set aside. Discard skins.

4 In a saucepan over medium heat, melt butter. Add onion and cook 3 to 5 minutes, until softened. Stir in roasted garlic, potato, bay leaf and thyme. Add stock and bring to a simmer. Reduce heat to medium-low and cook for 20 minutes, until potato is very tender. Remove and discard bay leaf.

5 In batches, transfer to blender or a food processor fitted with the metal blade (or use an immersion blender) and purée until smooth. Return to saucepan, if necessary, over medium heat. Stir in cream and salmon and season to taste with salt and pepper. Heat for 2 to 3 minutes, until warmed through. (Do not allow the soup to boil.)

6 Ladle into warm bowls and sprinkle with croutons to taste. (You may have some left over.) Serve immediately.

TIPS

For the creamiest result, use yellow-fleshed potatoes.

You can prepare this soup ahead of time. Once it's puréed, cover and refrigerate for up to 2 days. Just before serving, stir in the cream and salmon and heat until the soup is hot but not boiling.

Cajun seasoning is a salt, spice, herb and vegetable blend. Mixtures vary by brand. It may include black pepper, cayenne, thyme and oregano, as well as dried garlic and brown sugar. Buy a kind that specifies no MSG has been added.

Substitute an equal quantity of tuna, mackerel, crab, oysters or mussels for the salmon.

SALMON, CORN AND HERB CHOWDER WITH PEPPER JACK

MAKES ABOUT 7 CUPS (1.75 L) — 4 TO 6 SERVINGS • Creamy chowders tend to be bland. The addition of pepper Jack cheese livens up this one.

Blender or food processor

1 tbsp (15 mL) extra virgin olive oil

1 onion, diced

2 potatoes (about 12 oz/375 g), peeled and cut in 1-inch (2.5 cm) chunks (see Tip, below)

4 cups (1 L) chicken or vegetable stock

1 can (7½ oz/213 g) salmon, drained, deboned and broken into chunks

1 cup (250 mL) corn kernels

2 tbsp (30 mL) chopped parsley leaves

2 tbsp (30 mL) chopped chives

1 tbsp (15 mL) tarragon leaves, chopped

1 tbsp (15 mL) chopped dill fronds

2 tsp (10 mL) thyme leaves, chopped

1 cup (250 mL) half-and-half (10%) cream or whole milk

Salt

1 cup (250 mL) shredded pepper Jack cheese (4 oz/125 g)

1 In a large saucepan, heat oil over medium heat until shimmery. Add onion and cook, stirring often, for 3 to 5 minutes, until softened. Stir in potatoes and stock. Increase heat to medium-high and bring to a simmer. Reduce heat to medium-low and simmer for about 15 minutes, until potatoes are tender.

2 In batches, transfer to a blender or food processor fitted with the metal blade (or use an immersion blender) and purée. Return soup to saucepan, if necessary, over medium-low heat and stir in salmon, corn, parsley, chives, tarragon, dill and thyme. Simmer for 5 minutes, stirring often. Stir in cream or milk and simmer for 1 minute, until soup is very hot (do not allow it to boil). Season to taste with salt.

3 Ladle into warm bowls and sprinkle cheese over top, dividing equally.

TIP

Yellow-fleshed potatoes are best for this recipe. They give the soup a pleasant creaminess without potentially becoming gluey, like waxy red potatoes, or grainy, like russets.

Substitute an equal quantity of tuna, mackerel, crab, clams, oysters or mussels for the salmon.

CLAMS IN HERB BROTH WITH ANGEL HAIR PASTA

MAKES 4 SERVINGS • Is this a soup or a pasta? Well, it's both and neither. Definitions aside, you are sure to enjoy this vivid green, hot, comforting dish.

Mini blender or food processor

1 clove garlic

1 cup (250 mL) loosely packed coarsely chopped parsley leaves, divided

½ cup (125 mL) loosely packed coarsely chopped chives, divided

¼ cup (60 mL) loosely packed fresh dill fronds, divided

2 tbsp (30 mL) coarsely chopped tarragon leaves, divided

1 tbsp (15 mL) thyme leaves, divided

¼ cup (60 mL) extra virgin olive oil

½ tsp (2 mL) salt (approx.)

⅛ tsp (0.5 mL) freshly ground black pepper

2¼ cups (550 mL) chicken or vegetable stock, divided

1 bottle (8 oz/240 mL) clam juice

¼ tsp (1 mL) hot pepper flakes

1 can (5 oz/142 g) surf or meaty clams, rinsed, drained and coarsely chopped

4 oz (125 g) angel hair pasta

1 Bring a large pot of salted water to a boil over high heat.

2 In mini blender or food processor fitted with the metal blade, with the motor running, add garlic through the feed tube to chop. Scrape down the sides of the bowl. Add half each of the parsley, chives, dill, tarragon and thyme, and olive oil, salt and pepper. Process until smooth and light green. If necessary, add 2 tbsp (30 mL) stock to loosen the purée. Set aside.

3 In a saucepan, combine stock, clam juice, remaining parsley, chives, dill, tarragon, thyme and hot pepper flakes. Bring mixture to a simmer over medium-high heat. Reduce heat to medium-low and simmer for 10 minutes, until herbs are soft. Add clams and simmer for 5 minutes.

4 Meanwhile, add pasta to the boiling water and cook over medium heat for about 5 minutes, until tender to the bite (al dente). Drain.

5 Divide the pasta among 4 warmed large bowls and ladle soup over top. Serve the garlic-herb purée alongside for diners to stir into the soup.

Substitute an equal quantity of crab for the clams. Firm surf clams work best in this, but baby clams make an acceptable substitute.

NEW ENGLAND CLAM CHOWDER

MAKES ABOUT 6 CUPS (1.5 L) — 4 TO 6 SERVINGS • It's white versus red in the clam chowder popularity contest, and the former, known as New England clam chowder, is winning. It appeared first, in the mid-1800s, and has a thick, creamy white base. I have sampled clam chowders all over Cape Cod and in Boston. They always seem bland, stodgy and — dare I say it? — gluey. This one is not. Many New England chowder recipes call for heavy cream, but I prefer to use lighter cream and less flour.

- 1 cup (250 mL) water
- 1 bottle (8 oz/240 mL) clam juice
- 4 red potatoes (about 1 lb/500 g), peeled and cut in ½-inch (1 cm) dice
- 1 can (5 oz/142 g) surf clams, rinsed, drained and chopped
- 1 bay leaf
- 4 slices bacon, chopped
- 1 onion, diced
- 1 stalk celery, cut in small dice
- 2 cloves garlic, minced
- 2 tbsp (30 mL) all-purpose flour
- 1 tbsp (15 mL) dry sherry
- 2 tsp (10 mL) finely grated lemon zest
- ½ tsp (2 mL) salt (approx.)
- ¼ tsp (1 mL) freshly ground white pepper
- 1 cup (250 mL) table (18%) or half-and-half (10%) cream
- 1 to 2 tbsp (15 to 30 mL) chopped fresh dill fronds

1 In a large saucepan over medium-high heat, bring water, clam juice, potatoes, clams and bay leaf to a simmer. Reduce heat to low, cover and simmer for 10 minutes, until potatoes are tender. Place a sieve over a bowl and drain, reserving broth and solids separately. Discard bay leaf.

2 In the same saucepan over medium heat, cook bacon for 5 minutes, until browned and crisp. Using a slotted spoon, transfer to a plate lined with paper towels. Drain off all but 2 tbsp (30 mL) bacon drippings.

3 Heat drippings over medium-low heat. Add onion, celery and garlic and cook, stirring often, for 4 to 5 minutes, until softened. Sprinkle in flour. Cook, stirring, for 1 minute. Gradually stir in reserved broth, mixing until no lumps remain. Add reserved solids, sherry, lemon zest, salt and pepper. Reduce heat to low and simmer for 5 minutes, until celery is tender-crisp.

4 Stir in cream and dill to taste. Add salt to taste if necessary. Sprinkle reserved bacon over top and serve immediately.

Substitute an equal quantity of tuna, salmon, mackerel, crab, oysters or mussels for the clams. If you're substituting salmon or another flaky fish, add it at the end.

MANHATTAN CLAM CHOWDER

MAKES ABOUT 8 CUPS (2 L) — 6 TO 8 SERVINGS • Tomatoey Manhattan clam chowder is more of an acquired taste than its New England relative — but also way less calorific. Culinary historians theorize that Portuguese immigrants created this classic, even though adding tomatoes to clam chowder was widely reviled. In 1939 a bill making the practice illegal was even introduced in the Maine legislature! Manhattan chowder was not actually invented in New York; it was so named because supposedly only New Yorkers were crazy enough to eat it. I beg to differ.

4 slices bacon, chopped

4 red potatoes (about 1 lb/500 g), cut in ½-inch (1 cm) dice

1 stalk celery, thinly sliced on the diagonal

1 carrot, cut into matchsticks

1 onion, diced

¼ bulb fennel, diced (about ¾ cup/175 mL)

¼ green bell pepper, cut into matchsticks

2 cloves garlic, minced

¼ cup (60 mL) dry white wine

2 cups (500 mL) chicken stock

1 cup (250 mL) bottled clam-tomato cocktail

1 bottle (8 oz/240 mL) clam juice

1 can (5 oz/142 g) surf clams, rinsed, drained and chopped

1 cup (250 mL) canned diced tomatoes, with juice

4 sprigs thyme

¼ tsp (1 mL) salt (approx.)

⅛ tsp (0.5 mL) freshly ground black pepper

¼ cup (60 mL) chopped parsley leaves

Hot pepper sauce

1 In a large saucepan over medium heat, cook bacon for 5 minutes, until browned and crisp. Using a slotted spoon, transfer to a plate lined with paper towels to drain.

2 You should have about 2 tbsp (30 mL) drippings in the pan. Add potatoes, celery, carrot, onion, fennel, green pepper and garlic. Cook over medium-low heat, stirring often, for 10 minutes, until softened. Stir in wine. Stir in stock, clam-tomato cocktail, clam juice, clams, tomatoes, thyme, salt and pepper. Bring to a simmer over medium-high heat. Reduce heat to low, cover and simmer until vegetables are tender, 15 to 20 minutes.

3 Remove thyme sprigs and discard. Adjust salt to taste. Add parsley and reserved bacon. Dash liberally with hot pepper sauce. Serve immediately.

TIPS

Tangy clam-tomato cocktail is the not-so-secret ingredient in this recipe. It's sold in the supermarket's shelf-stable juice section.

Don't tell the clam chowder police I said so, but this tastes good with grated Parmesan.

FAUX PHO

MAKES 4 LARGE SERVINGS • Craving Vietnamese soup? This version is faster to make than traditional Vietnamese pho, which nowadays is a staple meal for college kids and diners on a budget.

4 oz (125 g) snow peas, trimmed and halved lengthwise (about 1½ cups/375 mL)

8 oz (250 g) thin (⅛ inch/3 mm) rice noodles

1 can (6 oz/170 g) boneless, skinless salmon, drained and broken into chunks

6 oz (175 g) bean sprouts (about 2½ cups/625 mL)

2 green onions (white and light green parts), thinly sliced on the diagonal

¼ cup (60 mL) loosely packed cilantro leaves

¼ cup (60 mL) loosely packed basil leaves, thinly sliced

Asian Stock (see Tips, below)

Asian chili sauce

1 lime, cut in 4 wedges

1 Bring a large pot of salted water to a boil over high heat. Add snow peas and blanch for 1 minute, until tender-crisp. Using a mesh scoop, transfer to a colander and rinse under cold running water to stop the cooking. Drain.

2 Add noodles to the boiling water and cook for about 5 minutes, until cooked through but not mushy. Drain. Rinse briefly under cold running water to stop the cooking. Drain.

3 Divide noodles among 4 warmed wide bowls. Top with equal amounts of salmon, snow peas, bean sprouts, green onions, cilantro and basil.

4 Reheat the stock over high heat until steamy but not boiling. Ladle into the bowls. Add a dollop of chili sauce to each bowl (or serve it alongside). Place a lime wedge on the edge of each bowl. Before eating, squeeze the lime into the soup and stir the ingredients together.

TIP

ASIAN STOCK: In 1 tbsp (15 mL) vegetable oil over medium heat, cook 1 small diced onion, 1 clove minced garlic and 4 thin slices of ginger, for about 3 minutes, or until softened. Add 5 cups (1.25 L) stock and 1 cup (250 mL) water. When liquid comes to boil, reduce heat to medium-low and simmer for 10 minutes, until onion is tender. Discard ginger. Stir in 2 tbsp (30 mL) soy sauce and 1 tbsp (15 mL) each fish sauce and hoisin sauce. Season with salt.

Substitute clams for the salmon. If using meaty clams, simmer in the stock with the onion and add equal amounts to the serving bowls along with the stock.

SOBA NOODLES WITH FISHBALLS AND SNOW PEAS

MAKES 4 SERVINGS • This Japanese-style soup tastes good, looks good and is good for you.

Rimmed baking sheet, lined with generously greased foil

FISHBALLS

1 can (7½ oz/213 g) salmon, drained, deboned and broken into chunks

1 egg

2 tbsp (30 mL) panko bread crumbs

1 small clove garlic, minced

1½ tsp (7 mL) unsalted butter, melted and cooled, optional

1 tsp (5 mL) finely grated lemon zest

1 tsp (5 mL) finely chopped cilantro leaves

½ tsp (2 mL) finely grated gingerroot

Pinch salt

Pinch freshly ground white pepper

SOUP

8 oz (250 g) soba noodles (see Tips, page 57)

6 cups (1.5 L) chicken or vegetable stock

4 oz (125 g) snow peas, trimmed and halved lengthwise (about 1½ cups/375 mL)

1 small carrot (about 2 oz/60 g), shredded (about ½ cup/125 mL)

4 shiitake mushrooms (about 2 oz/60 g), stemmed and sliced (see Tip, page 57)

4 slim green onions (white and light green parts), cut in 1-inch (2.5 cm) segments

2 tbsp (30 mL) ponzu sauce (see Tips, page 57)

Preheat oven to 350°F (180°C)

1 FISHBALLS: Gently squeeze salmon to remove excess moisture and place in a bowl. Add egg, panko crumbs, garlic, butter, if using, lemon zest, cilantro, ginger, salt and pepper. Using a fork, mash salmon and mix well.

2 With greased hands, shape salmon mixture into 1-inch (2.5 cm) balls and place on prepared baking sheet as completed (you should have about 18). Bake in preheated oven for 10 minutes. Turn and bake for 10 minutes more. Remove from oven and set aside for 5 minutes to firm up.

3 SOUP: In a large pot of boiling salted water over medium heat, cook noodles until tender but firm, about 10 minutes. Drain and rinse briefly under cold running water to remove excess starch. Drain.

4 Meanwhile, in a saucepan, bring stock to a simmer over high heat. Reduce heat to medium, add snow peas and carrot, and simmer for 3 minutes, until tender-crisp. Add mushrooms and onions. Simmer for 1 minute, until just tender. Remove from heat and stir in ponzu.

5 Divide noodles among 4 warmed serving bowls. Add fishballs and ladle hot soup over top.

TIPS

Soba are thin buckwheat noodles, which are very popular in Japan and catching on in other parts of the world. Ponzu is a citrus soy sauce. Both are sold in specialty shops and supermarkets with a good Asian section.

Fishballs have a tendency to become dry. The butter makes them moister, but this recipe will work fine without it.

Shiitake mushroom stems are too fibrous and tough to be edible. To remove them, just twist, pinch and pull them gently off the cap. If "waste not" is your mantra, use the stems to flavor stock before discarding them.

VARIATIONS

Substitute an equal quantity of shelled edamame for the snow peas. Simmer for 5 minutes.

Substitute Japanese udon (thicker wheat noodles) for the soba. Adjust the cooking time by following the package instructions.

CRAB, WATERCRESS AND EGG DROP SOUP

MAKES ABOUT 5 CUPS (1.25 L) — 4 SMALL SERVINGS • This comfort food looks pretty, and when you are sick — or just sick of winter's cold — it really hits the spot.

4 cups (1 L) low-sodium chicken or vegetable stock, divided

1 tbsp (15 mL) cornstarch

1 large egg

1 tsp (5 mL) toasted sesame oil

1 clove garlic, minced

1 tsp (5 mL) finely grated gingerroot

1 can (4.25 oz/120 g) crabmeat, rinsed and drained

2 cups (500 mL) watercress leaves, coarsely chopped

Salt and freshly ground black pepper

Asian hot chili oil, optional

1 In a small measuring cup, stir together ½ cup (125 mL) stock and the cornstarch.

2 In a small bowl, lightly whisk together egg and sesame oil.

3 In a saucepan over medium-high heat, bring remaining 3½ cups (750 mL) stock, garlic and ginger to a simmer. Reduce heat to medium-low and simmer for 2 minutes. Give the cornstarch mixture a big stir and whisk into the stock mixture in a slow, steady stream. Heat, stirring often, for 1 to 2 minutes, until mixture returns to a simmer and thickens, raising the heat if necessary. Stir in crab and watercress.

4 Hold the bowl with the egg mixture a few inches above the surface of the soup. With one hand, slowly pour in the egg, using a fork in the other hand to draw wide circles on the surface of the soup, catching the egg mixture and separating it into thin threads. Season to taste with salt and pepper.

5 Ladle into warm bowls and serve with chili oil alongside, if using.

TIPS

Adding 1 tsp (15 mL) oil per egg prevents stringy, spongy blobs in your egg drop soup. Instead, the strands will be silky and even.

You can use less expensive crab leg and flaked crabmeat for this soup.

Substitute an equal quantity of salmon or clams for the crab.

THAI COCONUT CRAB SOUP

MAKES ABOUT 4 CUPS (1 L) — 4 SMALL SERVINGS • Thai soup made with coconut milk is deliciously popular and takes to all kinds of seafood.

3 cups (750 mL) chicken or vegetable stock	1 Thai bird's-eye chile pepper, thinly sliced
4 fresh wild lime leaves (see Tips, below)	2 tbsp (30 mL) chopped cilantro leaves
1 stalk lemongrass, trimmed and chopped	1 tbsp (15 mL) shredded basil leaves (see Tips, below)
1 tbsp (15 mL) chopped gingerroot	1 can (4.25 oz/120 g) crabmeat, rinsed and drained
1 can (14 oz/400 mL) coconut milk	1 tbsp (15 mL) freshly squeezed lime juice
2 tbsp (30 mL) fish sauce (approx.), divided	Salt
2 green onions (white and light green parts), sliced	

1 In a medium saucepan over medium-high heat, bring stock, lime leaves, lemongrass and ginger to a simmer. Reduce heat to medium-low and simmer, uncovered, for 15 minutes. Place a sieve over a large bowl and strain soup. Discard solids and return liquid to saucepan.

2 Add coconut milk, 1 tbsp (15 mL) fish sauce, green onions, chile pepper, cilantro and basil to pan. Bring to a simmer over medium heat. Reduce the heat to medium-low and simmer for 5 minutes. Stir in crab and simmer for 1 minute, until heated through. Stir in lime juice. Taste and add up to 1 tbsp (15 mL) additional fish sauce, if desired. Season to taste with salt.

TIPS

You can use flaked crabmeat, but chunks are nicest in this soup. Buy shelf-stable crabmeat in a can or use part of a 1 lb (440 g) container of the better-quality pasteurized crabmeat.

To shred basil leaves, place them in a pile, roll them up like a cigar and slice thinly crosswise.

Wild lime leaves, sometimes called makrut lime leaves, are sold in Asian grocery stores and well-stocked supermarkets.

Substitute an equal quantity of salmon or mackerel for the crab.

SOUPS

CREAMY CRAB AND POBLANO SOUP

MAKES ABOUT 5 CUPS (1.25 L) — 4 SERVINGS • Poblanos are relatively mild Mexican peppers, but they still pack a punch in this addictive creation. You could add almost any seafood to the creamy base.

Blender or food processor

2 poblano peppers

2 tbsp (30 mL) unsalted butter

1 onion, diced

2 cloves garlic, chopped

1 potato, peeled and cut into 1-inch (2.5 cm) chunks (see Tips, below)

3 cups (750 mL) chicken or vegetable stock

½ cup (125 mL) chopped red bell pepper

½ cup (125 mL) half-and-half (10%) cream

¾ cup (175 mL) canned lump crabmeat (about 4 oz/125 g), rinsed and drained

Salt and freshly ground black pepper

¼ cup (60 mL) chopped cilantro leaves

4 lime wedges

Preheat broiler

1 Place poblano peppers on a baking sheet and broil, turning 2 to 3 times, until skin on all sides is blackened, about 25 minutes. Transfer to a paper bag and fold the top closed. When they are cool enough to handle, use a small, sharp knife to lift off the skins. Discard skins, core and seeds. Cut into ½-inch (1 cm) pieces. Set aside.

2 Meanwhile, in a saucepan, melt butter over medium heat. Add onion and garlic and cook, stirring often, for about 3 minutes, until softened. Stir in potato and stock and bring to a simmer over medium-high heat. Reduce heat to medium-low and simmer for about 15 minutes, until potato is tender.

3 In batches, transfer to blender or food processor fitted with the metal blade (or use an immersion blender) and purée. Return to saucepan, if necessary, and place over medium-low heat. Stir in bell pepper and simmer for about 5 minutes, until just tender. Stir in cream, reserved poblano peppers and crab. Heat the mixture for 1 minute but do not allow it to boil. Season to taste with salt and pepper.

4 Ladle into warm bowls and garnish with cilantro. Serve with lime wedges to squeeze into the soup.

TIPS

To easily remove seeds from sticky roasted peppers, dip the pieces briefly into a bowl of cold water.

Yellow-fleshed potatoes are best for this recipe. They give the soup a pleasant creaminess without becoming gluey, like waxy red potatoes, or grainy, like russets.

Lump crabmeat is best in this recipe. You can use part of a 1 lb (440 g) container of pasteurized crab or a 4.25 oz (120 g) can of shelf-stable chunk crabmeat.

Substitute an equal quantity of tuna, salmon, mackerel or clams for the crab.

Salads

Vintage Tuna Salad	64
Tuna Salad Three Ways	66
Classic Salmon Salad	68
Crab Louis	69
Tuna Cobb Salad	71
Tuna and Bean Salad on Arugula	72
Tuna Taco Salad	73
Thai Tuna Salad	74
Tuna, Egg and Fresh Bean Salad	75
Italian Tuna, Potato and Green Bean Salad	76
Sardines Caprese	77
Salade Niçoise	78
California Salmon Salad	80
Caesar Salad Two Ways	82
Retro Tuna Pasta Salad	84
Couscous with Tuna, Feta and Lemon Mint Dressing	85

VINTAGE TUNA SALAD

> **MAKES ABOUT 1 CUP (250 ML)** • Tuna salad is a brown-bag, lunch counter and cafeteria mainstay for kids and grownups alike. This vintage version is made with tried-and-true ingredients. If you want to experiment, try the variations on pages 66 and 67.

¼ to ⅓ cup (60 to 75 mL) mayonnaise

1 to 2 tbsp (15 to 30 mL) finely chopped sweet pickles, patted dry

1 tbsp (15 mL) finely diced celery (see Tips, below)

1 tbsp (15 mL) finely diced red onion

1 can (6 oz/170 g) chunk tuna in water, drained and broken into flakes

Salt and freshly ground black pepper

1 In a medium bowl, combine mayonnaise and pickles to taste, celery and onion. Gently squeeze tuna to remove excess moisture and add it to the bowl. Blend with a fork. Season to taste with salt and pepper.

2 Serve immediately or cover and refrigerate for up to 3 days.

TIPS

You'd think tuna salad would be the perfect place to use the cheaper flaked tuna, since everything is smooshed together. Nope. I recommend chunk tuna because it's less likely to turn into a paste.

Weepiness is tuna salad's number one preventable problem. Before using, drain the tuna in a sieve, flake it with your fingers and gently squeeze out excess moisture. Avoid watery additions such as chopped tomato or cucumber. The mayonnaise you choose also plays a role. If you use lower-fat mayonnaise, the tuna salad will become a bit looser and more watery after sitting, but the calorie savings make it worthwhile.

I prefer to use the tender inner stalks of celery known as the heart. You can, however, tenderize an outside stalk by peeling it.

VARIATION

Go upscale by using premium tuna in olive oil, drained. It is silkier and tastes richer, and you won't need as much mayonnaise.

Substitute an equal quantity of salmon, mackerel, sardines or crab for the tuna.

TUNA SALAD

Even if kids don't like fish, chances are they'll like tuna. Canned tuna was introduced to North Americans circa 1903, and tuna salad appeared not long afterward. It is the sandwich maker's Old Faithful — even more popular than its cousin, salmon salad. It is really a spread, of course, named back in the days when a few bits of chopped vegetables and mayonnaise made something a "salad." Versatile tuna salad is much more than a sandwich filling, however. You can mound it onto greens or rice to make a meal, spread it on crackers, or stuff it into celery boats or tomato cups.

TUNA SALAD THREE WAYS

Italian Tuna Salad

MAKES ABOUT 1 CUP (250 ML) • Tuna salad is a North American classic, but when I feel like updating and experimenting, I give it an international twist. For instance, pesto and sun-dried tomato add an Italian accent to this version. As with the original, it is very versatile.

¼ to ⅓ cup (60 to 75 mL) mayonnaise	½ tsp (2 mL) basil pesto
4 large pimiento-stuffed green olives, finely chopped and patted dry	1 can (6 oz/170 g) chunk tuna in water, drained and broken into flakes (see Tips, below)
1 oil-packed sun-dried tomato, drained and finely chopped (about 1 tbsp/15 mL)	Salt and freshly ground black pepper

1 In a bowl, combine mayonnaise to taste, olives, tomato and pesto. Gently squeeze tuna to remove excess moisture and add to the bowl. Blend with a fork and season to taste with salt and pepper.

2 Serve immediately or cover and refrigerate for up to 3 days.

TIP

I recommend using chunk tuna when making tuna salad because the end result is less likely to be pasty. Also, inexpensive flaked tuna sometimes tastes tinny.

In any tuna salad, you can substitute an equal quantity of salmon, mackerel, sardines or crab.

Indian Tuna Salad

> **MAKES ABOUT 1 CUP (250 ML)** • Indian curry paste and mango chutney bring spice and sweetness to tuna salad. Try spreading this version on warm naan bread or add a dollop atop rice for a quick meal.

¼ to ⅓ cup (60 to 75 mL) mayonnaise	1 tsp (5 mL) finely chopped cilantro leaves
1 tbsp (15 mL) finely diced yellow onion	1 can (6 oz/170 g) chunk tuna in water, drained and flaked (see Tip, page 66)
1 tsp (5 mL) mango chutney	
½ tsp (2 mL) prepared curry paste (see Tip, below)	Salt and freshly ground black pepper

1 In a bowl, combine mayonnaise to taste, onion, chutney, curry paste and cilantro. Gently squeeze tuna to remove excess moisture and add to the bowl. Blend with a fork and season to taste with salt and pepper.

2 Serve immediately or cover and refrigerate for up to 3 days.

TIP

Supermarkets sell a wide variety of Indian curry pastes, from mild to hot. I prefer Patak's Madras hot curry paste, but you can use your favorite kind.

Greek Tuna Salad

> **MAKES ABOUT 1 CUP (250 ML)** • Classic Greek accents, including olives and mint, make this tuna salad deliciously different. Stuff it into pitas or add it to Greek salad to make a meal.

¼ to ⅓ cup (60 to 75 mL) mayonnaise	¼ tsp (1 mL) finely grated lemon zest
4 kalamata olives, pitted, chopped and patted dry	1 can (6 oz/170 g) chunk tuna in water, drained and broken into flakes (see Tip, page 66)
1 tbsp (15 mL) finely chopped green bell pepper	
1 tbsp (15 mL) finely diced red onion	Salt and freshly ground black pepper
1 tsp (5 mL) finely chopped mint leaves	

1 In a bowl, combine mayonnaise to taste, olives, green pepper, onion, mint and lemon zest. Gently squeeze tuna to remove excess moisture and add to the bowl. Blend with a fork and season to taste with salt and pepper.

2 Serve immediately or cover and refrigerate for up to 3 days.

CLASSIC SALMON SALAD

MAKES ABOUT 1 CUP (250 ML) • Salmon salad is lovely when the fish is mixed with its classic partners, lemon and dill. Spread it on toasted artisan bread, add a scoop to dressed salad greens or even warm noodles, or use it as a filling for baked potatoes.

¼ to ⅓ cup (60 to 75 mL) mayonnaise

1 green onion (white and light green parts), finely chopped

1 tbsp (15 mL) finely chopped fresh dill fronds

1 tbsp (15 mL) sweet green relish

1 tsp (5 mL) finely grated lemon zest

1 can salmon (7½ oz/213 g), drained, deboned and broken into flakes

Salt and freshly ground black pepper

1 In a bowl, mix mayonnaise to taste, onion, dill, relish and lemon zest. Gently squeeze salmon to remove excess moisture and add it to the bowl. Blend with a fork. Season to taste with salt and pepper.

2 Serve immediately or cover and refrigerate for up to 3 days.

TIP

Use lower-fat or regular mayonnaise, as you prefer.

VARIATIONS

Omit the dill and relish, and add 2 tbsp (30 mL) finely chopped dill pickle, patted dry.

Substitute an equal quantity of lime zest for the lemon.

Substitute an equal quantity of tuna, mackerel, sardines or crab for the salmon.

CRAB LOUIS

MAKES 4 SERVINGS • You can't go wrong with this simple idea: crabmeat topped with spicy mayo and accompanied by tomato and egg. It's called Crab Louis, or the King of Salads. It started appearing on tony West Coast menus at the beginning of the twentieth century. Eateries in both San Francisco and Seattle lay claim to inventing it.

LOUIS SAUCE

½ cup (125 mL) mayonnaise

2 tbsp (30 mL) prepared tomato-based chili sauce

2 small green onions (white and light green parts), minced

1 tbsp (15 mL) finely chopped green bell pepper

Salt and freshly ground black pepper

SALAD

6 cups (1.5 L) shredded iceberg lettuce

1½ cups (375 mL) lump crabmeat (8 oz/250 g; see Tips, below)

4 large eggs, hard-cooked and quartered

4 cocktail tomatoes, quartered (see Tips, below)

1 tbsp (15 mL) capers, rinsed, drained and finely chopped

4 small lemon wedges

1 LOUIS SAUCE: In a measuring cup, stir together mayonnaise, chili sauce, green onions and bell pepper. Season to taste with salt and pepper. Set aside.

2 SALAD: Line shallow serving bowls with lettuce. Place crabmeat in the center and dollop Louis Sauce over top. Arrange eggs and tomatoes around crab. Scatter capers over top and place a lemon wedge in each bowl.

TIPS

For the best presentation, use larger lump crabmeat.

Bonus: This chili mayonnaise perks up all kinds of seafood.

Campari tomatoes are generically known as cocktail tomatoes and are sold in supermarkets. You can substitute 8 halved cherry tomatoes for the Camparis.

VARIATION

Add steamed asparagus spears.

Substitute an equal quantity of tuna or salmon for the crab.

TUNA COBB SALAD

MAKES 4 TO 8 SERVINGS • Cobb salad is an iconic dish that originated at Hollywood's Brown Derby restaurant. It is a composed salad, which means it is artfully arranged in layers or sections rather than tossed. In this variation, canned fish replaces the usual chicken breast. It makes a good-looking light meal — show it off in a clear bowl. I like to use thin homemade French dressing because it's not gloppy.

- 4 strips bacon, chopped
- 3 cups (750 mL) coarsely chopped iceberg lettuce
- 3 cups (750 mL) coarsely chopped romaine lettuce
- 1 to 1½ cups (250 to 375 mL) watercress leaves
- 1 small Belgian endive (about 3 oz/90 g), thinly sliced
- 4 cans (each 3 oz/85 g) solid tuna in olive oil, drained and broken into chunks
- 12 large cherry tomatoes (about 8 oz/250 g), quartered
- 1 ripe but firm avocado, cut in small dice (see Tip, below)
- 2 large eggs, hard-cooked and coarsely chopped
- 1 oz (30 g) blue cheese, crumbled (about ¼ cup/60 mL)
- 2 tbsp (30 mL) chopped chives
- Homemade French Dressing (see Tip, below)

1 In a skillet over medium heat, cook bacon for about 5 minutes, until browned and crisp. Using a slotted spoon, transfer to a plate lined with paper towels. Set aside.

2 Toss lettuces, watercress to taste, and endive in a large serving bowl. Scatter tuna, then tomatoes over top. Arrange avocado around the perimeter and scatter chopped egg in the center. Top with cheese, then chives. Scatter bacon over top. Drizzle dressing over the salad or serve it alongside (you will have some left over).

TIP

HOMEMADE FRENCH DRESSING: Whisk together ⅓ cup (75 mL) white wine vinegar, 1 clove garlic, minced, 2 tsp (10 mL) granulated sugar, ½ tsp (2 mL) each Worcestershire sauce, sweet paprika, mustard powder and salt, ¼ tsp (1 mL) freshly ground pepper and ¾ cup (175 mL) vegetable oil.

Substitute salmon, mackerel, sardines, sprats or crab for the tuna.

TUNA AND BEAN SALAD ON ARUGULA

MAKES 4 SERVINGS • During the big blackout of August 2003, we didn't have power for almost a week. This was one of the nourishing no-cook meals I prepared during that challenging time.

DRESSING

2 tbsp (30 mL) oil drained from tuna (approx.)

1 tsp (5 mL) oil drained from sun-dried tomatoes (approx.)

1 to 2 tbsp extra virgin olive oil (15 to 30 mL)

2 tbsp (30 mL) freshly squeezed lemon juice

1 clove garlic, minced

2 tsp (10 mL) chopped oregano leaves

½ tsp (2 mL) Dijon mustard

¼ tsp (1 mL) salt (approx.)

⅛ tsp (0.5 mL) freshly ground black pepper

SALAD

1 can (14 to 19 oz/398 to 540 mL) cannellini (white kidney) beans, rinsed and drained

4 green onions, sliced

2 stalks celery heart with leaves, sliced on the diagonal

2 oil-packed sun-dried tomatoes, drained (oil reserved) and finely chopped

2 cans (each 3 oz/85 g) tuna in olive oil, drained (oil reserved) and broken in chunks

1 small bunch arugula, trimmed and torn into bite-sized pieces

1 DRESSING: Pour oils from tuna and tomatoes into a measuring cup. Add extra virgin olive oil to equal ¼ cup (60 mL). Add lemon juice, garlic, oregano, mustard, salt and pepper. Whisk well.

2 SALAD: In a bowl, combine beans, onions, celery and sun-dried tomatoes. Pour dressing over top and toss gently. Cover and marinate for 30 minutes at room temperature. Add tuna and toss. Adjust salt to taste.

3 Line a serving dish or individual bowls with arugula. Spoon bean mixture over top. Serve immediately.

TIP

Celery hearts are the tender inner stalks. They are best in salads.

VARIATION

Substitute chopped or baby spinach for the arugula.

Substitute an equal quantity of salmon for the tuna.

TUNA TACO SALAD

MAKES 4 SERVINGS • Taco salad made with fish is better for you than one made with beef, because it is lower in saturated fat. This version makes a satisfying meal for kids and grownups.

2 tbsp (30 mL) extra virgin olive oil, divided

1 small onion, diced

1 clove garlic, minced

1 cup (250 mL) chopped canned tomatoes, with juices

1 cup (250 mL) cooked red kidney beans, rinsed and drained

1 tsp (5 mL) chili powder

½ tsp (2 mL) ground cumin

¼ tsp (1 mL) salt (approx.)

Freshly ground black pepper

3 cups (750 mL) shredded iceberg lettuce

2 plum tomatoes, cut in ¼-inch (0.5 cm) dice

¼ English cucumber, quartered lengthwise and thinly sliced

¼ cup (60 mL) diced red onion

1 tbsp (15 mL) freshly squeezed lime juice

8 cups (2 L) tortilla chips (about 6 oz/175 g)

1 can (6 oz/170 g) tuna in water, drained and broken into chunks

1 cup (250 mL) shredded Monterey Jack cheese (4 oz/125 g)

½ cup (125 mL) sour cream

2 tbsp (30 mL) chopped pickled jalapeño peppers

1 In a skillet, heat 1 tbsp (15 mL) oil over medium heat until shimmery. Add onion and garlic and cook, stirring, for 1 to 2 minutes, until onion softens. Stir in canned tomatoes, with juices, and cook for 1 minute. Add beans, chili powder, cumin, salt and freshly ground pepper. Reduce heat to medium-low, cover and simmer for 15 minutes, until mixture thickens.

2 Meanwhile, in a large bowl, combine lettuce, plum tomatoes, cucumber and red onion. Add lime juice and remaining 1 tbsp (15 mL) oil. Add salt, if necessary, and pepper to taste. Toss well.

3 Pile tortilla chips on individual serving plates. Top with lettuce mixture, tuna, cheese and warm bean mixture, dividing equally. Place a dollop of sour cream on each and scatter with jalapeños. Serve immediately.

Substitute an equal quantity of salmon for the tuna.

THAI TUNA SALAD

MAKES 4 TO 6 SERVINGS • One evening I was eating a classic Thai beef salad for dinner and thought, wow, this would be great with seafood. And it is, with only minimal changes.

DRESSING

2 to 3 tbsp (30 to 45 mL) freshly squeezed lime juice

2 tbsp (30 mL) toasted sesame oil (see Tips, below)

1 tbsp (15 mL) fish sauce

2 tsp (10 mL) soy sauce

2 tsp (10 mL) finely grated gingerroot (see Tips, below)

2 cloves garlic, minced

SALAD

4 cans (each 3 oz/85 g) solid tuna in olive oil, drained and broken into chunks

1 English cucumber, scrubbed, halved lengthwise and sliced

1 lb (500 g) cherry tomatoes, halved

1 cup (250 mL) sliced red onion

2 to 4 red Thai bird's-eye chile peppers, thinly sliced

Salt

1 cup (250 mL) lightly packed cilantro leaves

1 cup (250 mL) lightly packed torn basil leaves

½ cup (125 mL) roasted peanuts, coarsely chopped

1 DRESSING: In a small measuring cup, whisk together 2 tbsp (30 mL) lime juice, sesame oil, fish sauce, soy sauce, ginger and garlic. Taste and, if desired, whisk in remaining 1 tbsp (15 mL) lime juice. (The mixture should be tart.)

2 SALAD: Place tuna in a small, airtight container. Add half of the dressing. Cover and refrigerate for 1 hour, turning or shaking the container occasionally.

3 In a large, shallow serving bowl, combine cucumber, tomatoes, onion and chile peppers to taste. Add remaining dressing to taste and toss. Season to taste with salt. Scatter tuna mixture over top. Sprinkle cilantro and basil over top, then sprinkle on peanuts.

TIPS

Toasted sesame oil is also known as Asian sesame oil.

Grate ginger using a kitchen rasp such as the kind made by Microplane.

Use red chiles so you can see them. The green ones would be like hidden bombs in this salad.

Substitute an equal quantity of salmon for the tuna.

TUNA, EGG AND FRESH BEAN SALAD

MAKES 4 SERVINGS • Sometimes the simplest pleasures are the best, such as this down-to-earth, nourishing dinner salad.

Steamer

DRESSING

2 tbsp (30 mL) oil drained from tuna (approx.)

2 tbsp (30 mL) extra virgin olive oil (approx.)

2 tbsp (30 mL) white wine vinegar

1 tbsp (15 mL) chopped fresh basil leaves

½ tsp (2 mL) Dijon mustard

¼ tsp (1 mL) salt (approx.)

¼ tsp (1 mL) freshly ground black pepper

SALAD

1 lb (500 g) mixed green and yellow wax beans, trimmed

Salt

4 large leaves leaf lettuce

2 cans (each 3 oz/85 g) tuna in olive oil, drained (oil reserved) and broken into chunks

4 eggs, hard-cooked and halved or quartered

¼ cup (60 mL) finely chopped red onion

1 DRESSING: Pour oil from the tuna into a small measuring cup. Add enough extra virgin olive oil to equal ¼ cup (60 mL). Whisk in vinegar, basil, mustard, salt and pepper.

2 SALAD: Over a pan of simmering water, steam beans for about 10 minutes, until tender-crisp. Transfer to a colander and rinse under cold running water to stop the cooking.

3 Transfer beans to a medium bowl and add dressing. Toss well. Add salt to taste, if necessary.

4 Line a serving platter or individual bowls with lettuce. Arrange beans over top, dividing equally. Scatter tuna over beans, dividing equally. Arrange eggs around the edges and scatter onion over top. Serve immediately.

TIP

If you don't have a steamer, cook the beans in boiling salted water for about 5 minutes, until tender-crisp, or cook them in a microwave oven.

Substitute salmon or mackerel for the tuna.

ITALIAN TUNA, POTATO AND GREEN BEAN SALAD

MAKES 4 TO 6 SERVINGS • This salad is one example of the many ways Europeans appreciate tinned fish. The tuna makes it substantial, yet it still tastes light and fresh because it is tossed with dressing instead of mayonnaise.

8 oz (250 g) green beans, trimmed and halved (about 2 cups/500 mL)	1 stalk celery heart, cut in small dice
4 potatoes, scrubbed (about 1 lb/500 g)	2 tbsp (30 mL) chopped celery leaves
Salt	2 tbsp (30 mL) chopped basil
Lemon Dressing (see Tip, below)	1 tbsp (15 mL) chopped parsley leaves
2 cans (each 3 oz/85 g) solid tuna in olive oil, drained (oil reserved) and broken into chunks	12 black olives, pitted and halved

1 In a pot of boiling salted water, cook beans over medium heat for about 5 minutes, until tender-crisp. Using a mesh scoop, transfer to a colander. Rinse under cold running water to stop the cooking. Drain.

2 Add potatoes to the same pot of water and return to a boil. Cook for 15 to 20 minutes, until tender but firm. Transfer to a colander and drain, then rinse under cold running water to stop the cooking. When potatoes are cool enough to handle, peel and slice into rounds ½ inch (1 cm) thick.

3 Arrange potato slices on a serving plate in overlapping rows. Drizzle with 2 tbsp (30 mL) dressing and sprinkle lightly with salt. Top with tuna, then celery, then beans. Drizzle with additional dressing.

4 In a small bowl, toss together celery leaves, basil and parsley. Scatter mixture over salad. Scatter olives over top. Set assembled salad aside at room temperature for 10 minutes before serving, to meld flavors.

TIP

LEMON DRESSING: Drain the oil from the tuna into a small measuring cup. Add enough extra virgin olive oil to equal ¼ cup (60 mL). Whisk in 2 tbsp (30 mL) freshly squeezed lemon juice, 1 small clove garlic, minced, ½ tsp (2 mL) salt and ¼ tsp (1 mL) freshly ground black pepper.

Substitute salmon or mackerel for the tuna.

SARDINES CAPRESE

MAKES 4 SERVINGS • Simple Caprese salad, which comes from the isle of Capri, is the epitome of sunny Mediterranean flavors. Sardines are also a favorite in the region, so why not combine the two? Serve this with crusty bread to mop up the tangy juices, of which there are plenty.

2 ripe tomatoes (each 8 to 10 oz/ 250 to 300 g), cored and cut into ½-inch (1 cm) slices

8 oz (250 g) buffalo mozzarella, drained and cut into ¼-inch (0.5 cm) slices

10 large basil leaves

1 tin (3.75 oz/106 g) sardines, drained and cut in half lengthwise

2 tbsp (30 mL) extra virgin olive oil

1 tbsp (15 mL) balsamic vinegar

1 clove garlic, minced

¼ tsp (1 mL) salt

⅛ tsp (0.5 mL) freshly ground black pepper

1 Place sliced tomatoes on platter or individual serving plates. Top each slice with a similar-sized piece of mozzarella, a basil leaf and a sardine half, skin side up.

2 In a small bowl, whisk together oil, vinegar, garlic, salt and pepper. Drizzle over the tomato stacks. Serve immediately.

TIP

If you have premium olive oil, now is the time to use it, to make the Mediterranean flavors shine.

VARIATIONS

Buffalo mozzarella is pricy. If you prefer, use less expensive alternatives such as fior de latte, which is made with cow's milk, or even the firmer bocconcini balls.

On a platter you can create a traditional overlapping pattern, alternating the ingredients in circles instead of stacking them.

Substitute an equal quantity of tuna, salmon or mackerel for the sardines. Use one large chunk per stack or flake and scatter it on overlapping ingredients.

SALADE NIÇOISE

> **MAKES 4 TO 8 SERVINGS** • This tuna and vegetable salad is the signature dish of the Mediterranean seaside city of Nice. It is authentic to use canned tuna in olive oil, not grilled fresh tuna. The French are adamant that the original included no cooked vegetables, but over the years potatoes have found their way in.

8 oz (250 g) green beans, trimmed and sliced in half crosswise (about 2 cups/500 mL)

8 mini red potatoes (about 12 oz/375 g)

Vinaigrette (see Tips, page 79)

4 canned artichoke hearts, drained and quartered (see Tips, page 79)

1 head Boston lettuce, separated into leaves

2 small ripe tomatoes, cut in wedges

2 mini cucumbers, thinly sliced

1 small red bell pepper, cut in ¼-inch (0.5 cm) strips

1 cup (250 mL) thinly sliced red onion

4 cans (each 3 oz/85 g) solid tuna in olive oil, drained

2 tsp (10 mL) capers, rinsed, drained and chopped

1 small sprig basil

4 large eggs, hard-cooked and quartered

4 anchovy fillets, halved lengthwise

16 niçoise or small black olives, pitted

1 Bring a large pot of salted water to a boil over high heat. Add beans, reduce heat to medium and cook for 3 to 4 minutes, until tender-crisp. Using a mesh scoop, transfer beans to a colander and rinse under cold running water to stop the cooking. Set aside to cool.

2 Return heat to high and add potatoes to the cooking water. Bring to a boil, reduce heat to medium and cook for about 15 minutes, until potatoes are tender but firm. Drain and cut into quarters. Transfer to a bowl and toss warm potatoes with 1 tbsp (15 mL) vinaigrette.

3 In a small bowl, toss artichokes with 1 tbsp (15 mL) vinaigrette.

4 Line a large serving platter with lettuce. Arrange beans, potatoes, artichokes, tomatoes, cucumbers, red pepper and onion over top, leaving a small space in the center. Mound tuna in the center. Scatter capers over tuna and garnish with basil. Place egg wedges at the corners and drape with anchovies. Scatter olives over top. Serve immediately, with remaining vinaigrette alongside.

TIPS

VINAIGRETTE: In a large measuring cup, whisk together $\frac{1}{4}$ cup (60 mL) white wine vinegar, 1 minced shallot, 1 tbsp (15 mL) chopped parsley leaves, 1 tsp (5 mL) Dijon mustard and $\frac{1}{2}$ tsp (2 mL) each salt and freshly ground black pepper. Gradually whisk in $\frac{1}{2}$ cup (125 mL) extra virgin olive oil, until blended and thickened.

You can substitute oil from the tuna (about $\frac{1}{4}$ cup/60 mL) for some of the extra virgin olive oil in the Vinaigrette.

If you prefer, use thawed frozen artichoke hearts.

Slim French beans (called haricots) are standard in this salad, but regular green beans are fine. Don't trim the cute little squiggles off the ends.

Substitute an equal quantity of salmon, mackerel, sardines or crab for the tuna.

CALIFORNIA SALMON SALAD

MAKES 4 SMALL SERVINGS • What is California salad, anyway? It usually involves tossing nuts and fruit with baby greens, but otherwise it seems to be a free-for-all. Walnuts and grapes add appealing texture and a pleasant sweet-and-sour effect to this surprising combination with salmon.

DRESSING
- ¼ cup (60 mL) mayonnaise
- 2 tbsp (30 mL) extra virgin olive oil
- ½ tsp (2 mL) Dijon mustard
- ⅛ tsp (0.5 mL) salt
- ⅛ tsp (0.5 mL) freshly ground black pepper
- 1 tbsp (15 mL) chopped parsley leaves
- 1 tbsp (15 mL) chopped basil leaves

SALAD
- 1 can (6 oz/170 g) pink salmon, drained, deboned and broken into chunks
- ½ cup (125 mL) walnut pieces, toasted (see Tips, below)
- ½ cup (125 mL) seedless red grapes, quartered
- 3 green onions (white and light green parts), thinly sliced
- Salt
- 4 cups (1 L) mixed baby greens

1 DRESSING: In a measuring cup, whisk together mayonnaise, oil, mustard, salt, pepper, parsley and basil, until blended.

2 SALAD: In a bowl, combine salmon, walnuts, grapes and onions. Add dressing and toss to coat. Season to taste with salt.

3 Place greens on a serving platter or four individual dishes. Spoon salmon mixture over top. Serve immediately.

TIPS

The drier, less expensive pink salmon is fine for this because the mayonnaise moistens it.

Toast walnuts in a dry skillet over medium heat, shaking the pan often, for about 3 minutes, until fragrant and starting to brown. Transfer to a bowl to cool.

VARIATION

Stuff the salad into a pita or wrap and reduce the quantity of greens.

Substitute tuna for the salmon.

CAESAR SALAD TWO WAYS

MAKES 4 SERVINGS • Caesar salad must be North America's most popular restaurant, buffet and cafeteria salad. It gets its irresistible savoriness from anchovies and Parmesan cheese. When I crave Caesar salad, I start with this freeform recipe, then choose the dressing according to my mood. Add a topping, and dinner is served.

1 head romaine lettuce, leaves torn into bite-size pieces

Creamy Caesar Dressing or Caesar Vinaigrette (see below and page 83)

4 to 8 slices bacon, cooked crisp and crumbled

¼ to ½ cup (60 to 125 mL) freshly grated Parmesan cheese (½ to 1 oz/15 to 30 g)

Croutons

1. In a large bowl, toss romaine with dressing to taste.
2. Add bacon, Parmesan and croutons to taste. Toss lightly and serve immediately.

TIP

Here's an easy way to cook crispy bacon with less mess: Place four slices of bacon in a single layer on a ribbed microwave grill pan. If you don't have one, place the bacon on a microwave-safe plate lined with a paper towel. Cover the bacon with another paper towel. Microwave it on High for 2 minutes. Turn, cover with a fresh paper towel and microwave until crispy, about 1 minute. For two slices of bacon, halve the time.

Creamy Caesar Dressing

MAKES ABOUT 1 CUP (250 ML) • If you crave a creamy Caesar salad without the fuss of making a mayonnaise dressing from scratch, here's a delicious compromise.

Food processor or blender

3 cloves garlic

¾ cup (175 mL) mayonnaise (see Tips, page 83, top)

3 anchovy fillets

2 tbsp (30 mL) extra virgin olive oil

¼ cup (60 mL) freshly grated Parmesan cheese (½ oz/15 g; see Tips, page 83, top)

1 tbsp (15 mL) freshly squeezed lemon juice

1 tsp (5 mL) Worcestershire sauce

½ tsp (2 mL) Dijon mustard

4 capers, rinsed and drained

1. In a food processor fitted with the metal blade, with the motor running, drop garlic through the feed tube to chop. (You can also do this in a blender.) Scrape down the sides of the bowl. Add mayonnaise, anchovies, olive oil, Parmesan, lemon juice, Worcestershire sauce, mustard and capers. Process until mixture is smooth.

TIPS

Using mayonnaise as a base instead of the traditional coddled egg is more convenient and safer if you have any concerns about your egg supply.

You can use lower-fat mayonnaise.

In dressings you can use 2 tbsp (30 mL) dry grated 100% Parmesan (sold in tubs) for $\frac{1}{4}$ cup (60 mL) of the freshly grated kind.

Caesar Vinaigrette

> **MAKES ABOUT 1¼ CUPS (300 ML)** • For a lighter-tasting, crunchier Caesar salad, I sometimes opt for a vinaigrette dressing. This one has all the traditional Caesar flavors.

2 anchovy fillets, minced (see Tips, below)	¼ tsp (1 mL) salt (approx.)
2 cloves garlic, minced	⅛ tsp (0.5 mL) hot pepper sauce
1 small shallot, minced	1 cup (250 mL) extra virgin olive oil
1 tbsp (15 mL) white wine vinegar	2 tbsp (30 mL) grated Parmesan cheese (½ oz/15 g; see Tips, below)
1 tsp (5 mL) Worcestershire sauce	
½ tsp (2 mL) freshly ground black pepper	

1. In a bowl, whisk together anchovies, garlic, shallot, vinegar, Worcestershire sauce, pepper, salt and hot pepper sauce. Whisk in olive oil, then Parmesan. Add salt to taste, if necessary.

TIPS

It's simpler and more efficient to mash anchovies with a fork instead of chopping them.

I prefer dry grated 100% Parmesan (the powdery kind sold in tubs) in vinaigrettes, as the result is less creamy. However, you can use ¼ cup (60 mL) freshly grated Parmesan if you prefer.

RETRO TUNA SALAD PASTA

MAKES 7 CUPS (1.75 L) — 6 TO 8 SERVINGS • A pinch of nostalgia is the secret ingredient in this salad. I used to make this when I was a kid. It may be old-fashioned, but members of my family, both young and old, still gobble it up.

- 8 oz (250 g) large pasta shells
- 1 can (6 oz/170 g) tuna in water, drained and broken into small chunks
- 1 stalk celery heart with leaves, cut in small dice (see Tips, below)
- ½ red bell pepper, cut in small dice
- ½ to ¾ cup (125 to 175 mL) diced red onion
- ½ cup (125 mL) chopped sweet pickles
- ½ cup (125 mL) mayonnaise
- Salt and freshly ground black pepper
- 1 tbsp (15 mL) chopped parsley leaves, optional

1 In a large pot of boiling salted water, cook pasta over medium heat for about 12 minutes, until tender to the bite (al dente). Drain and rinse under cold running water until it cools to room temperature. Drain well.

2 Transfer to a large serving bowl. Add tuna, celery, red pepper, onion to taste, and pickles. Toss. Add mayonnaise and season to taste with salt and pepper. Mix well. Sprinkle parsley, if using, over top. Serve immediately.

TIPS

I prefer to use the tender inner stalks of celery known as the heart.

Cover and refrigerate leftovers for up to 3 days. The pasta will soak up the mayonnaise as it sits in the fridge. Revive leftovers by stirring in a tiny bit of cream or hot water.

VARIATIONS

When tempted to embellish this salad, I add coarsely chopped pitted black olives.

If you think your family will eat all of this salad right after it is prepared, you can add diced tomato to taste. Do not add it if you expect to refrigerate the salad, because the tomato will develop an unappetizing texture.

Substitute an equal quantity of dill pickles for the sweet ones, and sliced green onions for the red ones.

Substitute an equal quantity of salmon or mackerel for the tuna.

COUSCOUS WITH TUNA, FETA AND LEMON MINT DRESSING

MAKES 4 SERVINGS • Couscous is a quick-cooking, wholesome carb. Made from granular semolina, couscous is akin to pasta but is used like a grain. It is good warm, cold or at room temperature.

- 2 cans (each 3 oz/85 g) tuna in olive oil, drained (oil reserved) and broken into chunks
- 2 tbsp (30 mL) extra virgin olive oil (approx.)
- 1 tbsp (15 mL) freshly squeezed lemon juice
- 1 tsp (5 mL) salt
- 1/8 tsp (0.5 mL) freshly ground black pepper
- 1 tbsp (15 mL) finely chopped mint leaves
- 1 1/4 cups (300 mL) chicken or vegetable stock
- 1 cup (250 mL) instant couscous (see Tip, below)
- 1 large tomato, cut in 1/4-inch (0.5 cm) dice
- 1/2 English cucumber, peeled and cut in 1/4-inch (0.5 cm) dice
- 1/2 red bell pepper, cut in 1/4-inch (0.5 cm) dice
- 1/2 cup (125 mL) thinly sliced red onion
- 4 oz (125 g) feta cheese, broken into small chunks (about 1 cup/250 mL)
- 2 tbsp (30 mL) slivered mint leaves

1 Pour oil from tuna into a small measuring cup. Add enough extra virgin olive oil to make 1/4 cup (60 mL). Whisk in lemon juice, salt, pepper and mint. Set aside.

2 In a saucepan over medium-high heat, bring stock to a boil. Add couscous in a steady stream, stirring constantly. When mixture returns to a simmer, immediately cover and remove from heat. Set aside for 5 minutes, until liquid has been absorbed.

3 Transfer couscous to a large serving bowl and let cool for 5 minutes. Add tomato, cucumber, red pepper, onion and reserved tuna. Toss gently with dressing. Scatter feta over top.

4 Garnish with slivered mint leaves. Serve at room temperature.

TIP

North America supermarkets sell instant couscous. Authentic Moroccan couscous (not instant) is cooked in a double pot called a couscoussière.

Substitute an equal quantity of salmon for the tuna.

Sandwiches & Wraps

Diner Tuna Melts	88
Tuna McMelts	89
Tuna Muffuletta Sandwiches	90
Pan Bagnat	93
Tuscan Tuna Rolls	94
Parmesan Tuna Sandwiches	95
Tuna and Artichoke Panini	96
Sardines on Toast with Herb Drizzle	97
Salmon, Avocado and Red Onion Club Sandwiches	98
Vintage Creamed Salmon on Toast	99
CBLT	100
Hungarian Cheese Spread on Rye	101
Anchovy Egg Salad, Tomato and Sprouts in Pitas	102
Nutty Salmon and Spinach Wraps	103
Fish Tacos	104
Salmon and Sprout Quesadillas	107
Seafood Summer Rolls	108

DINER TUNA MELTS

MAKES 4 SERVINGS • The tuna melt is so versatile it is more of an idea than a recipe. Here's an introductory version. You can experiment by using any type of bread or cheese, from marble rye to bagels and from Swiss to Brie. Made with pita bread, the tuna melt becomes a personal pizza. In the United Kingdom, melts are known as "toasties."

Baking sheet, nonstick or lined with parchment

2 tbsp (30 mL) mayonnaise (see Tips, below)	1 can (6 oz/170 g) chunk tuna in water, drained and broken into flakes
2 tbsp (30 mL) finely diced celery heart	Salt and freshly ground black pepper
1 tbsp (15 mL) finely chopped onion	2 English muffins, split
1 tsp (5 mL) finely chopped parsley leaves	4 thin slices tomato, optional
½ tsp (2 mL) freshly squeezed lemon juice	4 slices marble Cheddar cheese (each ¾ oz/22 g)

Preheat oven to 400°F (200°C)

1 In a bowl, stir together mayonnaise, celery, onion, parsley and lemon juice. Add tuna and blend with a fork. Season to taste with salt and pepper.

2 Lightly toast muffins. Spread tuna mixture over each half, dividing equally. Place on prepared pan and top with tomato, if using, then the Cheddar. Bake in preheated oven for 5 to 10 minutes, until the cheese melts.

TIP
Use lower-fat mayonnaise if you prefer.

Substitute an equal amount of salmon or mackerel for the tuna.

SANDWICHES & WRAPS

TUNA MCMELTS

MAKES 4 SERVINGS • In this twist on a certain fast-food chain's breakfast sandwiches, tuna replaces the ham. These are yummy, although the cheese is more wilted than melted.

4 egg rings, greased

1 can (6 oz/170 g) chunk tuna in water, drained and broken into flakes

2 tbsp (30 mL) mayonnaise

4 English muffins, split

2 tbsp (30 mL) unsalted butter (approx.), softened

4 large eggs

4 slices processed cheese singles (see Tips, below)

1 Gently squeeze excess moisture from tuna and place it in a bowl. Add mayonnaise and, using a fork, mash together. Set aside.

2 Toast muffin halves and spread with butter.

3 Heat a nonstick skillet over medium heat. Place egg rings in skillet and crack eggs into rings. Pierce yolks with a fork. Cook for about 3 minutes or until whites are firm but yolks are still slightly wet.

4 Meanwhile, spread tuna mixture over bottom halves of muffins. Lay cheese slices over tuna. Place on serving plates.

5 Slide a spatula under each egg ring, flip it and, if necessary, loosen edges with a knife to release the egg. Remove the rings and transfer eggs to muffins. Replace tops of muffins.

TIPS

If you prefer, after adding the cheese, heat the muffin halves in a microwave oven on High for 10 to 15 seconds to slightly melt the cheese.

Use the individually packaged cheese singles labeled "Cheddar-style."

If you don't have egg rings, use tuna or salmon cans with the tops and bottoms removed.

Here's a handy alternative to using egg rings if you are making just one or two of these sandwiches at a time: grease a 2-cup (500 mL) microwave-safe measuring cup. Crack an egg into it and pierce the yolk with a fork. Microwave the egg on Medium-High for 30 to 40 seconds, until the white is firm but the yolk is slightly wet, then let it sit for 10 seconds.

Substitute an equal quantity of salmon or mackerel for the tuna.

SANDWICHES & WRAPS

TUNA MUFFULETTA SANDWICHES

MAKES 4 TO 6 SANDWICHES • Fish goes wonderfully well with olive salad, which means you can easily transform the famous New Orleans muffuletta into a healthier dish by substituting fish for the traditional salami and ham. The hearty muffuletta sandwich was invented in 1906 by a Sicilian who ran Central Grocery, an Italian-American store in the city's French Quarter.

OLIVE SALAD

⅔ cup (150 mL) black olives, pitted and finely chopped

⅔ cup (150 mL) green olives, pitted and finely chopped (see Tips, page 91)

¼ cup (60 mL) pimientos, drained and chopped

¼ cup (60 mL) finely chopped red onion

3 cloves garlic, minced

1 anchovy, minced

⅓ cup (75 mL) chopped parsley leaves

2 tbsp (30 mL) chopped fresh oregano leaves

1 tbsp (15 mL) capers, rinsed, drained and chopped

¼ tsp (1 mL) freshly ground black pepper

½ cup (125 mL) extra virgin olive oil

SANDWICHES

1 foccacia loaf (about 6½ by 10½ inches/16 by 27 cm), cut in half horizontally

4 oz (125 g) provolone cheese, sliced (6 slices)

2 cans (each 6 oz/170 g) tuna in water, drained and broken into flakes

1 OLIVE SALAD: In an airtight storage container, using a fork, stir together black and green olives, pimientos, onion, garlic, anchovy, parsley, oregano, capers, pepper and olive oil. Cover and refrigerate for several hours or overnight to meld flavors.

2 SANDWICHES: Moisten bottom half of the loaf with a thin layer of olive salad. Layer on provolone, then tuna. Spread remaining olive salad over top. Replace the top half of the loaf.

3 Cut into 4 or 6 segments and serve immediately.

TIPS

Although kalamatas are traditionally used in the olive salad, I prefer the richness of crinkly black olives.

You can buy green olives that are already pitted, but black olives tend to be sold unpitted because they are riper and softer. Avoid the canned pitted black olives.

Don't overdo the chopping — you want olive salad, not paste.

VARIATIONS

Go upscale by choosing tuna in olive oil. Drain and reserve the oil and substitute it for some of the extra virgin olive oil in the salad.

You can make this using individual rolls instead of a whole loaf of bread.

Hot pepper flakes are good in this olive salad, or try chopped peperoncini for a kick. Add them to taste.

Substitute an equal quantity of salmon or mackerel for the tuna.

PAN BAGNAT

MAKES 4 TO 6 SERVINGS • This French sub is like a Salade Niçoise sandwich. Messy and delicious, it lives up to its name, which translates as "bathed bread." For something a little different, serve small slices as an appetizer.

Mini blender

1 baguette (about 12 oz/375 g)

Olive dressing (see Tip, below)

2 cans (each 3 oz/85 g) tuna in olive oil, drained (oil reserved) and broken into flakes

2 or 3 cocktail tomatoes, thinly sliced

Salt

1 piece (about 2 inches/5 cm) English cucumber, peeled, thinly sliced and patted dry

2 large eggs, hard-cooked and sliced

¼ cup (60 mL) thinly sliced red onion

2 canned or thawed frozen artichoke hearts, patted dry and thinly sliced

¼ small red bell pepper, thinly sliced

6 small Boston lettuce leaves

1 Cut baguette in half lengthwise. Remove enough bread from the center of each half to make room for the filling. Lay bottom half, cut side up, on a long sheet of plastic wrap.

2 Smear half of the dressing over cut side of bottom layer. Add tuna and tomatoes and sprinkle lightly with salt. Layer on cucumber, eggs, onion, artichokes, red pepper and lettuce. Smear remaining dressing over cut side of top portion. Place on top of filled baguette and press down lightly.

3 Pull up the plastic around the loaf and wrap tightly. Refrigerate for 30 minutes before serving. To serve, cut on the diagonal into 4 to 6 sections.

TIP

OLIVE DRESSING: In mini blender, combine olive oil from tuna plus enough extra virgin olive oil to make ¼ cup (60 mL). Add 12 pitted black olives, 1 tbsp (15 mL) rinsed, drained capers, 1 tbsp (15 mL) white wine vinegar, 1 tsp (5 mL) each anchovy paste and parsley leaves, ½ tsp (2 mL) Dijon mustard and ¼ tsp (1 mL) freshly ground black pepper.

Substitute an equal amount of salmon or sardines for the tuna.

TUSCAN TUNA ROLLS

MAKES 3 SANDWICHES • Load up on flavor and healthful fiber with these wholesome sandwiches. They feature signature Tuscan ingredients, including cannellini beans and extra virgin olive oil.

1 can (14 to 19 oz/398 to 540 mL) cannellini (white kidney) beans, drained and rinsed (see Tip, below)	3 crusty Italian sub-shaped buns (each about 6 inches/15 cm long), split
3 tbsp (45 mL) extra virgin olive oil, divided	1 can (6 oz/170 g) tuna in water, drained and broken in small chunks
1 tbsp (15 mL) white wine vinegar	⅓ to ½ cup (75 to 125 mL) thinly sliced red onion
Salt and freshly ground black pepper	2 cups (500 mL) torn arugula leaves

1 In a bowl, using a potato masher, mash beans, 1 tbsp (15 mL) oil, vinegar and salt and pepper to taste. (Do not mash the beans into a paste — you want some texture in the sandwich.)

2 Brush remaining 2 tbsp (30 mL) oil over cut sides of buns. Arrange bottom halves on a work surface and spread with bean mixture. Gently squeeze tuna to remove excess moisture and place equal amounts over the beans. Add onion to taste and arugula, dividing equally. Replace tops, cut in half and serve immediately.

TIP

I use a 19-ounce (540 mL) can of beans. If using a smaller can, you will end up with less filling. In that case, try filling two buns instead of three.

VARIATIONS

Go upscale with tuna in olive oil and substitute the oil it is packed in for the extra virgin olive oil.

Make 4 small sandwiches with smaller buns.

Increase your fiber intake by using whole wheat buns.

Substitute an equal quantity of salmon, mackerel or sardines for the tuna.

PARMESAN TUNA SANDWICHES

MAKES 2 SANDWICHES • Here's another great Italian twist on the iconic tuna salad sandwich.

¼ cup (60 mL) mayonnaise

3 tbsp (45 mL) freshly grated Parmesan cheese (about ½ oz/15 g)

1 tbsp (15 mL) chopped basil leaves

1 tsp (5 mL) freshly squeezed lemon juice

1 can (6 oz/170 g) tuna in water, drained and broken into chunks

2 small kaiser rolls (about 4 inches/10 cm in diameter) split

4 slices tomato

Salt and freshly ground black pepper

Extra virgin olive oil

1 In a bowl, stir together mayonnaise, Parmesan, basil and lemon juice. Gently squeeze tuna to remove excess moisture and add it to the bowl. Mix with a fork.

2 Lightly toast rolls. Slather tuna mixture over bottom halves. Top with tomato slices, dividing equally, and season to taste with salt and pepper. Brush olive oil over cut sides of tops and replace.

3 Cut sandwiches into halves and serve immediately.

TIPS

If you're brown-bagging this sandwich, pack the tomatoes separately.

Use a rasp to grate the Parmesan so it is fluffy.

Substitute an equal quantity of salmon for the tuna.

TUNA AND ARTICHOKE PANINI

MAKES 4 PANINI • Add fish to your panini-press repertoire with these easy sandwiches. Brown-baggers, take note: this sandwich is surprisingly appetizing the day after it's made. You can eat it cold or heat it up in a microwave or toaster oven.

4 cans (each 3 oz/85 g) tuna in olive oil, drained (oil reserved)	¼ cup (60 mL) parsley leaves
4 crusty rolls, split	¼ cup (60 mL) chopped basil leaves
4 slices mozzarella (about 4 oz/125 g), each cut in half, divided	1 jar (6 oz/170 g) marinated artichoke hearts, drained and chopped

Panini press, preheated to High

1 In a bowl, using a fork, lightly mash tuna.

2 Brush cut surfaces of rolls with oil from the tuna. Place bottoms on a work surface. Layer with half the mozzarella, all the parsley, basil, tuna and artichokes, and then the remaining mozzarella. Replace tops.

3 Place sandwiches on preheated panini press and cook for 3 to 5 minutes, until toasted and golden. Cut in half before serving.

TIPS

If you don't have a panini press, heat the sandwiches in a large skillet or grill pan. Preheat the pan and weigh the sandwiches down by placing a second hot skillet on top. If the sandwich is not toasting evenly, flip it.

Use crusty rolls with a soft crumb.

You can use lower-fat mozzarella.

Save the oil from the marinated artichoke hearts to make salad dressing.

Substitute an equal quantity of salmon or mackerel for the tuna.

SARDINES ON TOAST WITH HERB DRIZZLE

MAKES 2 SERVINGS • Turning sardines into a light meal is simple. As a kid in a Hungarian family, I happily munched on rye bread and sardines with a spritz of lemon. This is a tad more sophisticated but still fast and easy.

Mini food processor

1 cup (250 mL) parsley leaves

½ cup (125 mL) fresh dill fronds

1 tbsp (15 mL) freshly squeezed lemon juice

¼ tsp (1 mL) salt (approx.)

2 tbsp (30 mL) extra virgin olive oil

2 slices rye bread

Softened unsalted butter, optional

2 leaves Boston lettuce

2 tins (each 4 oz/120 g) boneless, skinless sardines, drained

1 In a 2-cup (500 mL) measure, combine parsley and dill. Add boiling water to cover. Immediately transfer to a fine-mesh sieve, drain and rinse under cold running water. Drain well and use the back of a spoon to squeeze out remaining moisture.

2 In mini food processor, pulse parsley and dill until chopped and blended. Add lemon juice, salt and oil, and process until smoothly blended. Adjust salt to taste.

3 Lightly toast the bread until golden and butter lightly, if desired. Place toast on individual serving plates and top each with a lettuce leaf. Arrange whole sardines over top. Drizzle 1 to 2 tbsp (15 to 30 mL) herb dressing over each, to taste.

TIP

This recipe makes about ¼ cup (60 mL) dressing. You can spoon leftovers over other canned or fresh fish or steamed vegetables.

Substitute an equal quantity of tuna, salmon, mackerel or crab for the sardines.

SALMON, AVOCADO AND RED ONION CLUB SANDWICHES

MAKES 2 SANDWICHES • The iconic triple-decker club sandwich has evolved considerably beyond its standard chicken and bacon filling. This version calls for salmon, but it also works with other seafood. Culinary historians date the club back to the late nineteenth century. They think it originated in country clubs or men's social clubs, particularly one gambling establishment for gentlemen in Saratoga Springs, New York.

4 slices bacon

¼ cup (60 mL) mayonnaise

1 tsp (5 mL) freshly squeezed lemon juice

2 tsp (10 mL) chopped parsley leaves

6 slices whole wheat bread

2 small leaves Boston lettuce

½ tomato, thinly sliced

Salt and freshly ground black pepper

½ ripe but firm avocado, thinly sliced

1 can (7½ oz/170 g) salmon, drained, deboned and broken into chunks

¼ cup (60 mL) thinly sliced red onion

1 In a skillet over medium-high heat, cook bacon for about 5 minutes, until browned and crisp. Transfer to a plate lined with paper towels to drain.

2 In a measuring cup, mix mayonnaise, lemon juice and parsley.

3 Toast bread until golden but not crisp. Arrange slices on a work surface in two sets of three. Lightly smear two slices with mayonnaise on one side only and smear the third slice on both sides. Repeat with second set.

4 Working with first set, with mayo side up, place lettuce leaf on bottom slice. Top with half of the bacon and 2 tomato slices (you will have some left over). Season to taste with salt and pepper. Top with half the avocado and the bread slice spread on both sides with mayo.

5 Mix salmon with remaining mayonnaise mixture. Spread half over top slice of bread. Arrange half the onion over salmon. Cover with third slice of bread, mayo side down, and press together gently. Repeat with second set of bread and remaining ingredients.

6 Cut each sandwich into 4 triangles and secure each with a toothpick.

Substitute an equal quantity of tuna for the salmon.

VINTAGE CREAMED SALMON ON TOAST

MAKES ABOUT 3 CUPS (750 ML) — 2 TO 4 SERVINGS • You may remember this dish as Salmon Wiggle, from the from the old expression "get a wiggle on," which means "hurry up." Early wiggles relied totally on canned ingredients — sometimes simply soup, salmon and peas — so the name is appropriate. This recipe is a bit fancier, but not by much. Salmon wiggle was a comforting childhood staple for many older folks, particularly in New England. Of course, there are plenty who recall tuna wiggle and shrimp wiggle too. Wiggle was ladled over toast, rice, noodles or even soda crackers. I prefer it over rice or noodles, but to each his or her own.

- 2 tbsp (30 mL) unsalted butter
- 1 leek (white and light green parts), thinly sliced
- ½ tsp (2 mL) salt (approx.)
- 1 clove garlic, minced
- ¼ cup (60 mL) dry white wine, optional
- 1¼ to 1½ cups (300 to 375 mL) whole milk
- 2 tbsp (30 mL) all-purpose flour
- 1 can (7½ oz/213 g) sockeye salmon, drained, deboned and broken into chunks
- 1 cup (250 mL) green peas, thawed if frozen
- Freshly ground white pepper
- 1 tbsp (15 mL) chopped parsley
- 4 lemon wedges
- 2 to 4 slices of bread, toasted

1 In a medium saucepan, melt butter over medium-low heat. Add leek and salt. Cook, stirring occasionally, for 8 to 10 minutes, until leek softens and turns golden. Stir in garlic for 20 seconds. Stir in wine, if using, and cook for 1 minute, until evaporated.

2 In a large measuring cup, whisk together 1¼ cups (300 mL) milk and the flour. Gradually add to leek, stirring constantly. When mixture comes to a simmer, reduce heat to low. Simmer for 2 minutes or until thickened. Stir in salmon and peas and season to taste with pepper. Cook, stirring often, for 5 minutes, until mixture is warmed through. Add some or all of the remaining milk to adjust the thickness, keeping in mind that the wiggle will loosen as it sits. Adjust salt to taste.

3 Sprinkle parsley over top and serve immediately, with lemon wedges alongside.

Substitute an equal quantity of tuna or mackerel for the salmon.

SANDWICHES & WRAPS

CBLT

MAKES 4 SANDWICHES • What could be better than a BLT? A CBLT — a crab, bacon, lettuce and tomato sandwich. Crab tossed with peppery lime mayonnaise takes this mainstay sandwich over the top.

Rimmed baking sheet
Wire rack

LIME MAYO

⅓ cup (75 mL) mayonnaise

1 tsp (5 mL) finely grated lime zest

1 tbsp (15 mL) freshly squeezed lime juice

⅛ tsp (0.5 mL) salt

¼ tsp (1 mL) freshly ground black pepper

SANDWICHES

12 slices bacon

8 slices white or whole wheat sandwich bread

4 small leaves Boston lettuce

2 tomatoes, thinly sliced

Salt

1½ cups (375 mL) crabmeat (8 oz/250 g), rinsed and drained (see Tips, below)

Preheat oven to 450°F (230°C)

1 LIME MAYO: In a measuring cup, stir together mayonnaise, lime zest and juice, salt and pepper.

2 SANDWICHES: Lay bacon on wire rack and place on baking sheet. Bake in preheated oven for 15 to 20 minutes, turning halfway through, until crisp. Transfer to a plate lined with paper towels and drain.

3 Toast bread until it is golden but not crisp. Lay 4 slices on a work surface. Smear each with a thin layer of lime mayo. Place 3 slices of bacon on each slice of bread. Top with 1 lettuce leaf and tomato slices, dividing equally. Season to taste with salt.

4 Squeeze the crab gently to remove excess moisture and transfer to a bowl. Add remaining lime mayo and stir gently. Spoon mixture over tomato slices and spread evenly. Top with remaining bread.

5 Cut each sandwich into 2 triangles and serve immediately.

TIPS

The oven is the best place to cook a large number of bacon slices without a big mess.

You can use two 4.25-oz (120 g) shelf-stable cans of chunk crabmeat or half of a 1-lb (440 g) container of pasteurized crab claw meat.

HUNGARIAN CHEESE SPREAD ON RYE

> **MAKES ABOUT 1⅓ CUPS (325 ML) — MAKES 10 TO 12 SERVINGS** • This classic Austro-Hungarian cheese spread is tangy and bold, thanks to the addition of anchovies. It is better known by its German name, Liptauer cheese, although there are many versions in different parts of Europe. Hungarians call it körözött. I loved this as a kid, and so did my own children. Mine is modernized with lemon juice to brighten the flavor and a lot less butter than my mom uses.

- 1 package (8 oz/250 g) pressed dry cottage cheese (see Tips, below)
- 2 tbsp (30 mL) unsalted butter, softened
- 3 green onions (white and light green parts), minced
- 4 anchovy fillets, minced
- 2 tbsp (30 mL) capers, rinsed, drained and finely chopped
- 1 tsp (5 mL) Dijon mustard
- 1½ tsp (7 mL) sweet paprika (approx.)
- ¼ tsp (1 mL) caraway seeds
- 1 to 2 tsp (5 to 10 mL) freshly squeezed lemon juice
- Salt
- 10 to 12 slices rye bread

1 In a bowl, using a fork, mash together cottage cheese and butter. Add green onions, anchovies, capers, mustard, paprika and caraway seeds. Add 1 tsp (5 mL) lemon juice and blend well. Add salt and additional lemon juice, if desired, to taste.

2 Transfer to an airtight container, cover and refrigerate for at least 1 hour to meld the flavors, or for up to 7 days. When you are ready to serve, toast bread until golden brown. Smear about 2 tbsp (30 mL) körözött over each slice. Sprinkle additional paprika lightly over top.

3 Cut each slice in half and serve immediately.

TIPS

In this recipe, do not use the large-curd, creamy cottage cheese sold in tubs, which is too wet. For the best texture and richer flavor, I use dry cottage cheese with 10% milk fat, but lower-fat versions will work too.

If you can't wait, you can enjoy this cheese spread immediately after making it. However, it is best once chilled.

This cheese spread keeps well in the fridge for a week, so you don't have to make all the sandwiches at once. Enjoy it at breakfast or lunch.

VARIATIONS

If you don't like caraway seeds, add a pinch of ground caraway.

Spread cheese on crackers for snacks and canapés.

You can substitute pickle juice for the lemon juice.

ANCHOVY EGG SALAD, TOMATO AND SPROUTS IN PITAS

MAKES 8 SANDWICHES • The anchovy and the egg are true soul mates. Together they make a lip-smacking savory sandwich filling.

- 8 large eggs, hard-cooked and coarsely chopped (see Tips, below)
- ¼ cup (60 mL) mayonnaise
- 8 anchovy fillets, minced
- 1 tsp (5 mL) Dijon mustard
- ¼ tsp (1 mL) sweet paprika
- ⅛ tsp (0.5 mL) freshly ground black pepper
- 4 whole wheat pocket pitas (about 6 inches/15 cm in diameter), halved
- 2 tomatoes, thinly sliced
- 1 package (2½ oz/70 g) onion sprouts

1. In a bowl, using a fork, mash eggs, mayonnaise, anchovies, mustard, paprika and pepper. You will have about 2¼ cups (550 mL) filling.

2. Place pitas on work surface. Spread a generous ¼ cup (60 mL) filling in each pita half. Insert tomato slices and stuff in sprouts. Serve immediately.

TIPS

Here's a carefree way to hard-cook eggs: Place the eggs in a small pan and cover with about ½ inch (1 cm) water. Heat on medium-high. When the water comes to a full boil, cover and immediately remove the pan from the heat. Let it stand for 10 minutes. Run cold water over the eggs until they are cool enough to handle. Peel them immediately (the shell is less likely to stick that way).

If you're brown-bagging this sandwich, prevent sogginess by packing the tomatoes separately.

VARIATIONS

Use your favorite type of sprouts, such as broccoli, alfalfa or onion sprouts, or substitute micro-greens such as broccoli, kale, radish or cabbage shoots.

NUTTY SALMON AND SPINACH WRAPS

MAKES 2 WRAPS • Nuts add a pleasant crunch to this herbed salmon salad, which is wrapped in a whole wheat tortilla. The result has a wholesome appeal.

¼ cup (60 mL) mayonnaise (see Tips, below)

2 green onions (white and green parts), finely chopped

½ tsp (2 mL) Dijon mustard

1 tbsp (15 mL) chopped basil leaves

1 tbsp (15 mL) chopped parsley leaves

1 can (7½ oz/213 g) salmon, drained, deboned and broken into chunks

¼ cup (60 mL) walnuts or pecans, toasted and chopped (see Tips, below)

2 tbsp (30 mL) dried cranberries, optional

Salt and freshly ground black pepper

2 small whole wheat tortillas (6½ inches/17 cm in diameter)

1 cup (250 mL) finely sliced spinach leaves

1 In a bowl, using a fork, stir together mayonnaise, green onions, mustard, basil and parsley. Gently squeeze salmon to remove excess moisture and add it to the bowl. Add walnuts and cranberries, if using, and mix well. Season to taste with salt and pepper.

2 Lay tortillas on a work surface and spread with salmon mixture, leaving a 2-inch (5 cm) border on the right. Top with spinach leaves. Fold up about 1 inch (2.5 cm) of bottom edge of each tortilla, then roll tightly from left to right. Lay seam side down on work surface.

3 Wrap each tightly in a napkin, leaving top exposed. Serve immediately.

TIPS

You can use lower-fat mayonnaise to keep the calorie count down.

Toast walnuts in a dry skillet over medium heat for about 3 minutes, until fragrant and turning golden.

Slice the spinach by stacking the leaves in a pile, rolling them up like a cigar and then cutting crosswise.

Substitute an equal quantity of tuna for the salmon.

FISH TACOS

> **MAKES 12 TACOS** • These are less calorific but just as messy cousins of Baja fish tacos. Usually made with fried battered fish and tortillas that are either fried or doubled up to prevent leaks, Baja fish tacos are San Diego's most famous dish. They were popularized in 1983 by chain restaurateur Ralph Rubio, who first enjoyed them a decade earlier in Mexico.

DRESSING

½ cup (125 mL) sour cream

½ cup (125 mL) mayonnaise

2 tbsp (30 mL) chopped cilantro leaves

1 tbsp (15 mL) minced chipotle chile pepper in adobo sauce

Salt

SALSA

3 small tomatoes (about 12 oz/ 375 g total), cut in ¼-inch (0.5 cm) dice

⅓ cup (75 mL) chopped sweet onion (such as Vidalia)

⅓ cup (75 mL) loosely packed cilantro leaves

1 small jalapeño pepper, seeded and chopped

1 clove garlic, minced

1 tbsp (15 mL) freshly squeezed lime juice

½ tsp (2 mL) salt (approx.)

¼ tsp (1 mL) freshly ground black pepper

TACOS

12 small corn tortillas (about 5½ inches/14 cm in diameter)

1½ cups (375 mL) finely shredded green cabbage (about 3 oz/90 g)

2 cans (each 6 oz/170 g) tuna in water, drained, excess moisture removed and broken into flakes (see Tips, page 106)

Preheat oven or toaster oven to 350°F (180°C)

1 DRESSING: In a measuring cup, stir together sour cream, mayonnaise, cilantro, chipotle pepper and salt to taste. You will have about 1 cup (250 mL) dressing.

2 SALSA: In a bowl, stir together tomatoes, onion, cilantro, jalapeño, garlic, lime juice, salt and pepper. Taste and adjust salt if necessary. You will have about 2 cups (500 mL) salsa.

3 TACOS: Divide tortillas into two batches and wrap each in foil. Place in preheated oven and heat for 10 to 12 minutes, until warm.

4 Place warm tortillas on a work surface. Smear each with about 1½ tbsp (22 mL) dressing and top with about 2 tbsp (30 mL) cabbage. Add about 2 tbsp (30 mL) tuna and, using a slotted spoon, about 2 tbsp (30 mL) salsa. (You will have some salsa left over.) Serve immediately.

continued on page 106

TIPS

Go upscale by using top-quality solid white albacore tuna in your Fish Tacos. Squeeze the tuna gently with your hands to remove excess moisture before using it.

These tacos are not rolled but rather presented open-faced, to be folded by the diner.

Bonus: This fresh salsa is also delightful with quesadillas, enchiladas or nachos, or served alongside grilled fish or chicken. Do not make the salsa ahead of time — refrigeration is disastrous for it because the cold ruins the texture of the tomatoes.

VARIATION

Substitute flour tortillas for the corn ones.

Catch of the Day: Substitute an equal quantity of salmon for the tuna.

SALMON AND SPROUT QUESADILLAS

MAKES 4 • You can't go wrong with quesadillas when the family's mealtime looms. These are fast, easy and popular with all ages.

8 whole wheat flour tortillas (7 inches/18 cm in diameter)

2 cups (500 mL) shredded smoked mozzarella (8 oz/250 g)

1 can (7½ oz/213 g) salmon, drained, deboned and broken into flakes

2 cups (500 mL) loosely packed onion or broccoli sprouts, divided

Vegetable oil or spray

¼ to ⅓ cup (60 to 75 mL) prepared salsa

¼ to ⅓ cup (60 to 75 mL) sour cream

Hot pepper sauce

1 Place 4 tortillas on a work surface. Scatter with half the mozzarella, dividing equally. Gently squeeze salmon to remove excess moisture and scatter it evenly over top. Set aside a small portion of sprouts for garnishing and scatter the remainder over salmon. Top with remaining cheese. Place remaining tortillas over top.

2 Heat a large skillet or griddle over medium heat. Brush or spray lightly with oil. Using a wide spatula, transfer quesadillas to pan and cook, in batches if necessary, for about 2 minutes per side, until cheese melts and tortillas are slightly crisp and marked by brown spots. If they are browning too quickly, reduce heat to medium-low. Transfer each to a serving plate as completed and keep warm.

3 When all the quesadillas are cooked, top each with a dollop each of salsa and sour cream and finish with a dash of hot sauce (you can also serve it alongside). Garnish with reserved sprouts and serve immediately.

TIP
You can also cook quesadillas in a panini press preheated to Medium.

VARIATION
Use any kind of sprouts or micro-greens you like.

Replace salmon with an equal quantity of tuna.

SEAFOOD SUMMER ROLLS

MAKES 8 ROLLS • Vietnamese summer rolls are so light compared to their fried cousins, spring rolls. Wrapped in thin rice paper, these uncooked rolls with greens are also known as salad rolls, fresh rolls or crystal rolls.

Lightly greased baking sheet

1 cup (250 mL) peeled, julienned English cucumber (about ½)

1 cup (250 mL) watercress leaves

½ cup (125 mL) cilantro leaves

½ cup (125 mL) coarsely chopped or torn basil leaves (see Tips, page 109)

½ cup (125 mL) thinly sliced green onions (4 to 6; white and light green parts)

¼ cup (60 mL) shredded carrot

8 rice paper wrappers, 8½ inches (22 cm) in diameter (see Tips, page 109)

Salt and freshly ground black pepper

2 cans (each 6 oz/170 g) boneless, skinless salmon, drained and broken into flakes

Dipping sauce (see Tips, page 109)

1. Place cucumber in a fine-mesh sieve and set aside to drain for at least 10 minutes. Pat dry just before using.

2. In a small bowl, toss together watercress, cilantro and basil. In another small bowl, stir together onions and carrot.

3. Fill a rimmed baking sheet or shallow container with warm water. Working with one wrapper at a time, submerge wrapper in water for 20 to 30 seconds, until softened all over. Lay flat on your work surface.

4. Place about 1½ tbsp (22 mL) onion mixture just below the centre of the wrapper. Top with about 1 tbsp (15 mL) cucumber. Season to taste with salt and pepper. Add about 2 tbsp (30 mL) salmon, spreading evenly over cucumber. Top with about ¼ cup (60 mL) watercress mixture. Fold edge of wrapper closest to you over filling. Fold sides toward the middle, then roll up tightly. Set, seam side down, on prepared baking sheet. Repeat with remaining wrappers and filling.

5. Serve immediately or place rolls under a damp cloth to keep moist. (The wrappers tend to dry out quickly.) To serve, cut each roll in half on the diagonal and serve dipping sauce alongside.

TIPS

DIPPING SAUCE: In a small bowl, stir together ¼ cup (60 mL) each freshly squeezed lime juice, fish sauce, water and granulated sugar, 1 tbsp (15 mL) shredded carrot and 1 thinly sliced Thai bird's-eye chile, if desired. Cover and refrigerate for at least 1 hour or overnight to develop flavors. (Makes about ⅔ cup/150 mL.)

Thin, dry rice paper is tricky to work with. Soak it just until it is pliable but not ready to disintegrate. Run your fingers over the wrapper to help it soak evenly. You should be able to pick it up and place it on the work surface without it breaking. If the water cools too much, refill the container. You will ruin a few wrappers before you get the hang of it, but they are not expensive.

Instead of chopping the basil, you can shred it by piling the leaves on top of each other, rolling them up together like a cigar and then slicing crosswise.

Substitute an equal quantity of tuna, mackerel or crab for the salmon.

SANDWICHES & WRAPS

Fish Burgers, Fish Cakes & More

• • •

Niçoise Tuna Burgers	112
Open Sesame Salmon Burgers	115
Salmon Burgers with Honey Ginger Mayo	116
Jerk Salmon Sliders	118
Thai Curry Salmon Burgers	120
Crabby Cakes	121
Tuna Croquettes	124
Salmon Loaf	126

NIÇOISE TUNA BURGERS

MAKES 4 BURGERS • The fixings put these fish burgers over the top, but you can also use the recipe to make generic tuna burgers and add your own touches.

Broiling pan, covered with generously greased foil

NIÇOISE MAYO

¼ cup (60 mL) mayonnaise

1 tbsp (15 mL) chopped marinated artichoke hearts

2 tsp (10 mL) finely chopped red onion

2 tsp (10 mL) finely chopped black olives (3 small)

½ tsp (2 mL) capers, drained and finely chopped

¼ tsp (1 mL) anchovy paste

1 large basil leaf, chopped

Salt

BURGERS

1 large egg

¼ cup (60 mL) mayonnaise (see Tips, page 113)

1 clove garlic, minced

1 tbsp (15 mL) prepared tomato-based chili sauce

1 tsp (5 mL) finely grated lemon zest

1 tsp (5 mL) finely chopped parsley leaves

2 cans (each 6 oz/170 g) tuna in water, drained and broken into chunks

½ cup (125 mL) panko bread crumbs (see Tips, page 113)

2 tbsp (30 mL) extra virgin olive oil, divided

4 small crusty buns, about 3½ inches (9 cm) in diameter, split

4 slices tomato

2 eggs, hard-cooked and sliced

Preheat broiler, placing oven rack one level down from top position

1 NIÇOISE MAYO: In a measuring cup, stir together mayonnaise, artichokes, onion, olives, capers, anchovy paste, basil and salt to taste. Set aside.

2 BURGERS: In a bowl, using a fork, mix egg, mayonnaise, garlic, chili sauce, lemon zest and parsley. Gently squeeze tuna to remove excess moisture and add to bowl. Add panko crumbs and mix well.

3 Divide tuna mixture into 4 portions, each about ½ cup (125 mL), and shape each into a patty approximately 3½ inches (9 cm) in diameter. Place on prepared pan as completed.

4 Brush tops of patties with half of the oil. Place under preheated broiler for about 5 minutes, until tops look golden and dry. Carefully turn over and brush with remaining oil. Return to broiler and broil for about 4 minutes, until flipsides look golden and dry. Set aside for 2 minutes to firm up.

5 Place patties on bottoms of buns and top with tomato and eggs. Slather Niçoise Mayo on cut sides of the top halves of buns and replace. Serve immediately.

TIPS

Panko is Japanese-style bread crumbs. Light yet crunchy, panko straddles the gap between standard dry bread crumbs and fresh bread crumbs. Most supermarkets sell panko, often in the sushi section.

To counteract dryness I add a bit of mayonnaise to fish burgers. Tuna needs more than salmon. Full-fat mayo is preferable but the lower-fat kind will work.

Be gentle with the patties. Use a spatula to lift them from your work surface or plate to the pan, and turn them carefully as they cook. I use two short-handled spatulas to turn them.

MAKING FISH BURGERS

- To counteract dryness I add a bit of mayonnaise, oil or butter to the mix when making fish burgers. Salmon needs less than tuna. Full-fat mayo is preferable but the lower-fat kind will work. Another potential moistener is sour cream.

- When making fish burgers, it's important to squeeze excess moisture from the fish to ensure that the mixture won't be too wet to handle. You should be able to gently pat the mixture into patties.

- I prefer to cook fish burgers under the broiler or on the grill rather than in a skillet, which increases the chances that they will crumble. If you're using the barbecue, place the burgers on greased foil rather than directly on the grate, which is a recipe for disaster.

- Be gentle with the patties. Use a spatula to lift them from your work surface or plate to the pan, and turn them carefully as they cook. I use two short-handled spatulas to turn them.

OPEN SESAME SALMON BURGERS

MAKES 4 BURGERS • Sesame lovers can get their fix with this Asian-inspired fish burger.

Broiling pan, covered with generously greased foil

1 large egg

2 tbsp (30 mL) mayonnaise

1 tbsp (15 mL) toasted sesame oil

2 tsp (10 mL) soy sauce

2 cans (each 6 oz/170 g) boneless, skinless salmon, drained and broken into chunks

½ cup (125 mL) panko bread crumbs (see Tips, below)

4 leaves leaf lettuce

4 sesame seed buns

Sesame Mayo (see Tips, below)

4 slices tomato

¼ cup (60 mL) thinly sliced red onion

Preheat broiler, placing oven rack one level down from top position

1 In a bowl, using a fork, mix egg, mayonnaise, sesame oil and soy sauce. Gently squeeze salmon to remove excess moisture and add to the bowl. Add panko crumbs and mix well.

2 Divide salmon mixture into 4 portions and shape each into a patty approximately 4½ inches (11.5 cm) in diameter. Place each on prepared pan as completed.

3 Place patties under preheated broiler for about 5 minutes, until tops are golden brown. Carefully turn over and broil for about 4 minutes, until flipside is golden brown. Remove from oven and set aside for 2 minutes to firm up.

4 Place lettuce on bottoms of buns and place patties on top. Slather patties with sesame mayo and top with tomato and onion. Replace tops of buns and serve immediately.

TIPS

SESAME MAYO: In a measuring cup, stir together ¼ cup (60 mL) mayonnaise, 2 tsp (10 mL) each toasted sesame oil and toasted sesame seeds, ½ tsp (2 mL) each finely grated lime zest and freshly squeezed lime juice, and ¼ tsp (1 mL) each soy sauce and Asian chili sauce, such as sambal oelek or sriracha.

Toast sesame seeds in a dry skillet over medium heat, shaking the pan often, for 2 to 3 minutes, until seeds start to clump and turn golden and fragrant. Immediately transfer to a bowl. Even easier, buy toasted sesame seeds, which are available in many supermarkets. For an attractive presentation, use toasted mixed white and black sesame seeds.

Panko is Japanese-style bread crumbs. Light yet crunchy, panko straddles the gap between standard dry bread crumbs and fresh bread crumbs. I highly recommend it. Most supermarkets sell panko, often in the sushi section.

See page 114 for additional tips on making fish burgers.

SALMON BURGERS WITH HONEY GINGER MAYO

MAKES 4 BURGERS • The touch of sweetness in this fragrant honey-spiked mayonnaise complements the salmon.

Broiling pan, covered with generously greased foil
Food processor

HONEY GINGER MAYO

¼ cup (60 mL) mayonnaise

2 tsp (10 mL) soy sauce

1 tsp (5 mL) honey

1 small clove garlic, minced

½ tsp (2 mL) finely grated gingerroot (see Tips, page 117)

BURGERS

2 slices stale whole wheat bread (about 2½ oz/70 g), torn into chunks

1 large egg

2 tbsp (30 mL) mayonnaise

2 tsp (10 mL) soy sauce

2 tsp (10 mL) chopped chives

1 tsp (5 mL) finely grated lime or lemon zest

⅛ tsp (0.5 mL) freshly ground black pepper

2 cans (each 7½ oz/213 g) pink salmon, drained, deboned and broken into chunks

4 multigrain flatbread burger buns, about 4½ inches (11 cm) in diameter (see Tips, page 117)

¼ cup (60 mL) thinly sliced red onion

½ cup (125 mL) watercress leaves or baby greens

Preheat broiler, placing oven rack one level down from top position

1 HONEY GINGER MAYO: In a measuring cup, stir together mayonnaise, soy sauce, honey, garlic and ginger. Set aside.

2 BURGERS: In food processor fitted with the metal blade, pulse bread 10 times, until medium crumbs form. You should have about 1½ lightly packed cups (375 mL; see Tips, page 117).

3 In a bowl, using a fork, mix egg, mayonnaise, soy sauce, chives, lime or lemon zest and pepper. Gently squeeze salmon to remove excess moisture and add to the bowl. Add bread crumbs and mix well.

4 Divide salmon mixture into 4 portions, each a generous ½ cup (125 mL), and shape each into a patty about 4 inches (10 cm) in diameter. Place on prepared pan as completed.

5 Place patties under preheated broiler for about 5 minutes, until tops are golden brown. Carefully turn over and broil for about 4 minutes, until flipside is golden brown. Remove from oven and set aside for 2 minutes to firm up.

6 Place patties on bottoms of buns and slather with the mayo. Top with onion and watercress or baby greens. Replace tops and serve immediately.

TIPS

It can be tricky to prepare burgers with canned fish. Since the fish is already cooked, the mixture doesn't naturally adhere together when heat is applied, so binders are necessary. I prefer to use egg and bread crumbs, fresh or dry, or sometimes mashed potato. Some cooks turn to dried potato flakes or cooked rice. You need to find a balance — just enough binder to make fish burgers, not bread burgers.

I like to use a kitchen rasp, such as the kind made by Microplane, to grate the gingerroot into a purée.

Fresh bread crumbs can vary wildly in volume, depending on how you put them in the measuring cup and how long they sit. As time passes, the volume diminishes because the crumbs dry out and settle. So if you have a kitchen scale, go by weight. I pulse the torn bread into medium crumbs — neither too coarse nor too fine. For a volume measure, I scrape the crumbs into a measuring cup but do not pack them down or rap the cup to get them to settle.

Flatbread burger buns, split horizontally, are sold in many supermarkets. You can, however, use any bun you like.

JERK SALMON SLIDERS

MAKES 8 SLIDERS • Sliders are miniature burgers that make great party fare. These sliders are tasty morsels for fans of spicy food.

Broiling pan, covered with generously greased foil

HERB LIME MAYO

¼ cup (60 mL) mayonnaise

1 small clove garlic, minced

2 tsp (10 mL) finely chopped parsley leaves

2 tsp (10 mL) finely chopped chives

1 tsp (5 mL) finely grated lime zest

Salt

BURGERS

1 large egg

2 tbsp (30 mL) mayonnaise

1 tbsp (15 mL) toasted sesame oil (see Tips, page 119)

2 green onions (white and light green parts), minced

2 tsp (10 mL) soy sauce

1 tsp (5 mL) finely grated lime zest

1 tsp (5 mL) finely chopped cilantro leaves

2 cans (each 7½ oz/213 g) salmon, drained, deboned and broken into chunks

½ cup (125 mL) panko bread crumbs (see Tips, page 119)

¼ cup (60 mL) prepared jerk sauce (see Tips, page 119)

8 slider buns, each about 2½ inches (6 cm) in diameter

8 slices plum tomato

Preheat broiler, placing oven rack one level down from top position

1 **HERB LIME MAYO:** In a measuring cup, stir together mayonnaise, garlic, parsley, chives, lime zest and salt to taste. Set aside.

2 **BURGERS:** In a bowl, using a fork, mix egg, mayonnaise, sesame oil, green onions, soy sauce, lime zest and cilantro. Gently squeeze salmon to remove excess moisture and add to the bowl. Add panko crumbs and mix well.

3 Divide salmon mixture into 8 portions, each a generous ¼ cup (60 mL), and shape each into a patty about 2½ inches (6 cm) in diameter. Place on prepared pan as completed.

4 Place patties under preheated broiler for 3 to 4 minutes, until tops look golden and dry. Brush with half the jerk sauce and broil for 1 minute. Carefully turn over and broil until flipsides look golden and dry, about 2 to 3 minutes. Brush with remaining jerk sauce and broil for 30 to 60 seconds. Remove from oven and set aside for 2 minutes to firm up.

5 Place patties on bottom halves of buns and top with tomato slices. Slather cut sides of tops with the mayo, replace tops and serve immediately.

TIPS

Toasted sesame oil, also known as Asian sesame oil, is made from toasted or roasted seeds. Dark and aromatic, it is sold in small bottles as a flavoring agent. Do not confuse toasted sesame oil with yellow sesame oil pressed from raw seeds.

Jamaican jerk sauce is made with hot peppers (particularly Scotch bonnet chiles) and aromatic spices. You can buy small jars at the supermarket.

For additional tips on making fish burgers, see page 114.

Panko is Japanese-style bread crumbs. Light yet crunchy, panko straddles the gap between standard dry bread crumbs and fresh bread crumbs. I highly recommend it. Most supermarkets sell panko, often in the sushi section.

If you prefer, grill fish burgers on the barbecue. For best results, mimic the broiling method, placing the burgers on greased foil, not directly on the grate.

THAI CURRY SALMON BURGERS

MAKES 4 BURGERS • Curry accents work nicely with the salmon in these fish burgers. The topping, a Thai version of tartar sauce, adds the fresh flavors of basil and lemon.

Broiling pan, covered with generously greased foil

1 large egg
2 tbsp (30 mL) mayonnaise
2 tbsp (30 mL) coconut cream (see Tips, below)
2 tsp (10 mL) Thai green curry paste
1 small clove garlic, minced
¼ tsp (1 mL) dried basil
⅛ tsp (0.5 mL) freshly ground black pepper
2 cans (each 7½ oz/213 g) salmon, drained, deboned and broken into chunks
½ cup (125 mL) panko bread crumbs
4 leaves leaf lettuce
4 whole-grain flatbread burger buns, about 4½ inches (11.5 cm) in diameter (see Tips, below)
Basil Mayo (see Tips, below)

Preheat broiler, placing oven rack one level down from top position

1 In a bowl, using a fork, mix egg, mayonnaise, coconut cream, curry paste, garlic, basil and pepper. Gently squeeze salmon to remove excess moisture and add to the bowl. Add panko crumbs and mix well.

2 Divide salmon mixture into 4 portions, each a generous ½ cup (125 mL), and shape each into a patty about 4 inches (10 cm) in diameter. Place on prepared pan as completed.

3 Place patties under preheated broiler for about 5 minutes, until tops are golden brown. Carefully turn over and broil for about 4 minutes, until flipside is golden brown. Remove from oven and set aside for 2 minutes to firm up.

4 Place lettuce on bottoms of buns and place patties on top. Slather patties with the Basil Mayo, replace tops and serve immediately.

TIPS

BASIL MAYO: In a measuring cup, stir together ¼ cup (60 mL) mayonnaise, 1 tbsp (15 mL) sour cream, 1 small green onion, minced, 2 tsp (10 mL) chopped basil leaves, ½ tsp (2 mL) freshly squeezed lemon juice, and salt and freshly ground black pepper, to taste.

If you don't have coconut cream, scoop the separated "cream" off the top of a can of non-emulsified coconut milk. Do not mistake coconut cream for creamed coconut, which is sweetened and sold in blocks.

For additional tips on making fish burgers, see page 114.

I enjoy fish burgers in the thin specialty buns sold in many supermarkets. These small, round flatbreads, split horizontally, don't overwhelm the patty.

CRABBY CAKES

MAKES 8 • Canned crab is worth buying just for these tasty little treats. Crab cakes can be tricky to prepare, as they are best with as little binder as possible. I've added just enough egg and crumbs to hold them together.

Food processor

MINTY CUCUMBER DIP

½ cup (125 mL) finely chopped cucumber

¼ tsp (1 mL) salt (approx.)

1 cup (250 mL) Greek yogurt

1 tbsp (15 mL) freshly squeezed lime juice (see Tips, page 123)

1 tbsp (15 mL) chopped mint leaves

CRAB CAKES

2 slices stale white bread (about 2½ oz/70 g), torn into chunks

1 large egg

1 tbsp (15 mL) toasted sesame oil

1 tbsp (15 mL) freshly squeezed lime juice

1 small shallot, minced

1 clove garlic, minced (see Tips, page 123)

1 tbsp (15 mL) finely chopped red bell pepper

1 tsp (5 mL) chopped parsley leaves

¼ tsp (1 mL) ground ginger

¼ tsp (1 mL) salt

1½ cups (375 mL) canned crab claw meat (8 oz/250 g), rinsed and drained (see Tips, page 123)

Cornstarch

1 tbsp (15 mL) unsalted butter, optional

¼ cup (60 mL) vegetable oil for frying

1 DIP: In a fine-mesh sieve, toss cucumber with salt. Place over a bowl and set aside to drain for 10 to 15 minutes.

2 Squeeze excess moisture from cucumber and transfer to a small serving bowl. Add yogurt, lime juice and mint and stir to blend. Taste and adjust salt. Cover and refrigerate until chilled or for up to 2 days.

3 CRAB CAKES: In food processor fitted with the metal blade, pulse bread 10 times, until medium crumbs form. You should have about 1½ lightly packed cups (375 mL).

4 In a bowl, using a fork, mix egg, sesame oil, lime juice, shallot, garlic, red pepper, parsley, ginger and salt. Gently squeeze crab to remove excess moisture and add to bowl along with bread crumbs. Mix well.

5 Scatter cornstarch evenly and liberally over a large plate. Divide crab mixture into 8 portions. With greased hands, pat each mound into a ball, roll in the cornstarch to coat, then flatten slightly. Refrigerate, uncovered, for 15 to 30 minutes to firm up.

continued on page 123

6 In a large skillet, melt butter, if using, with oil over medium heat. Using a spatula, and with greased hands, transfer a patty to your palm. Gently flatten to ½ to ¾ inch (1 to 2 cm) and place in the hot oil. Repeat, in batches, with remaining patties, frying for 3 to 4 minutes a side and turning carefully when bottoms are golden brown and firm. (Lower the heat if they are browning too quickly.)

7 Set aside for 2 minutes to firm up. Serve warm, with Minty Cucumber Dip alongside.

TIPS

If you don't have Greek yogurt, spoon 1½ cups (375 mL) regular yogurt into a strainer lined with cheesecloth, place over a bowl, cover and refrigerate for 2 hours or until thickened and reduced to 1 cup (250 mL). Discard liquid in bowl.

Buy small lump crabmeat, as the flaked kind is not substantial enough for making patties. I prefer pasteurized claw meat because it has a fuller flavor and firmer texture. Coarsely chop any long claw pieces. You'll need half of a pound (500 g) container. If desired, double this crab cake recipe or use the remainder in other dishes.

For the finest minced garlic, push the clove through a garlic press.

Toasted sesame oil, also known as Asian sesame oil, is made from toasted or roasted seeds. Dark and aromatic, it is sold in small bottles as a flavoring agent. Do not confuse toasted sesame oil with yellow sesame oil pressed from raw seeds.

I use two small spatulas to carefully turn the crab cakes.

Adding a pat of butter to the frying oil adds buttery flavor to fish cakes.

To maintain more control over the final result, I always use unsalted butter in recipes. With salted butter, the amount of salt varies by brand. And salted butter contains more moisture, which can affect some recipes. Salt also masks rancidity.

Bottled reconstituted lemon and lime juices usually contain additives. That's why I always use freshly squeezed juice. I squeeze the whole lemon or lime and immediately store the leftover juice in a small tub in the fridge or freeze it in 1 tbsp (15 mL) portions in an ice cube tray.

VARIATIONS

The cornstarch makes the patties easier to work with, but if you prefer, use dry crumbs such as panko instead. Note that crab cakes with a panko coating will brown faster.

Substitute an equal quantity of full-fat mayonnaise for the sesame oil.

TUNA CROQUETTES

MAKES 8 • Fish cakes aren't pretty to look at but they taste pretty good. My family snatches them up before I can even get them onto serving plates. Minty Cucumber Dip is a refreshing accompaniment.

MINTY CUCUMBER DIP

½ cup (125 mL) finely chopped cucumber

¼ tsp (1 mL) salt (approx.)

1 cup (250 mL) Greek yogurt

1 tbsp (15 mL) freshly squeezed lime juice (see Tips, page 123)

1 tbsp (15 mL) chopped mint leaves

CROQUETTES

2 large eggs

1 can (6 oz/170 g) tuna in water, drained and broken into chunks

1 cup (250 mL) packed cold mashed potatoes (about 8 oz/250 g; see Tips, page 125)

1 tbsp (15 mL) honey Dijon mustard

1 tsp (5 mL) freshly squeezed lemon juice

1 large green onion (white and green parts), minced

1 tsp (5 mL) finely chopped fresh dill fronds

¼ tsp (1 mL) sweet paprika

¼ tsp (1 mL) salt

⅛ tsp (0.5 mL) freshly ground black pepper

¾ cup (175 mL) panko bread crumbs, divided (see Tips, page 125)

1 tsp (5 mL) dry Italian seasoning

1 tbsp (15 mL) unsalted butter, optional

¼ cup (60 mL) vegetable oil

1 DIP: In a fine-mesh sieve, toss cucumber with salt. Place over a bowl and set aside to drain for 10 to 15 minutes.

2 Squeeze excess moisture from cucumber and transfer to a small serving bowl. Add yogurt, lime juice and mint and stir to blend. Taste and adjust salt. Cover and refrigerate until chilled or for up to 2 days.

3 CROQUETTES: In a bowl, lightly whisk eggs. Gently squeeze tuna to remove excess moisture and add to bowl. Add potatoes, mustard, lemon juice, green onion, dill, paprika, salt and pepper. Mix well with a fork. Add ¼ cup (60 mL) panko crumbs. Refrigerate, uncovered, for 15 to 30 minutes.

4 Place remaining panko crumbs and Italian seasoning in a wide, shallow bowl. Crumble together with fingers.

5 Divide croquette mixture into 8 portions. With greased hands, shape each into a rough ball and roll in the crumbs to coat thoroughly. Pat into a disk about 3 inches (7.5 cm) in diameter.

6 In a skillet over medium heat, melt butter, if using, with oil. In batches, fry croquettes for 2 to 3 minutes a side, turning carefully when bottoms are golden brown and firm (turn down heat if they are browning too quickly).

7 Set aside for 2 minutes to firm up. Serve warm, with Minty Cucumber Dip alongside.

TIPS

If you don't have Greek yogurt, spoon 1½ cups (375 mL) regular yogurt into a strainer lined with cheesecloth, place over a bowl, cover and refrigerate for 2 hours or until thickened and reduced to 1 cup (250 mL). Discard liquid in bowl.

Tuna croquettes are a fine way to use up leftover mashed potatoes.

Before refrigeration, the tuna mixture should just hold together. To test it, press a small amount lightly in your hand — it should not crumble.

If your mashed potatoes are very moist, very dry or very buttery, you may have to experiment with the quantity of bread crumbs you add to the tuna mixture.

Panko bread crumbs are light and crispy. Most supermarkets sell panko; look for it in the sushi section or bakery department.

VARIATION

Save calories by baking your croquettes. Place them on a baking sheet lined with generously greased foil and bake in an oven preheated to 400°F (200°C) for 15 minutes, until bottoms are golden brown. Flip and bake for 10 minutes more, until other sides are golden brown.

Substitute an equal quantity of salmon, mackerel or crab for the tuna.

FISH BURGERS, FISH CAKES & MORE

SALMON LOAF

MAKES 6 TO 8 SERVINGS • Here's the canned-fish equivalent of meatloaf. For an easy family dinner, serve it with mashed potatoes and salad. Enjoy any leftovers by turning them into fishloaf sandwiches.

Food processor
Rimmed baking sheet
9- by 5-inch (23 by 12.5 cm) loaf pan, greased and lined with parchment sling (see Tips, page 127)

- 4 slices stale white bread (about 5 oz/150 g), torn
- 4 cans (each 7½ oz/213 g) salmon, drained, deboned and broken into chunks
- 4 large eggs
- ¼ cup (60 mL) mayonnaise
- 2 tsp (10 mL) finely grated lemon zest
- 2 tbsp (30 mL) freshly squeezed lemon juice
- 2 tsp (10 mL) Dijon mustard
- ½ cup (125 mL) chopped chives
- 2 tsp (10 mL) chopped fresh dill fronds
- ½ tsp (2 mL) salt
- ¼ tsp (1 mL) freshly ground black pepper

Preheat oven to 325°F (160°C)

1 In food processor fitted with the metal blade, pulse bread 10 to 12 times, until medium crumbs form. You should have about 3 cups (750 mL). Transfer to a rimmed baking sheet and toast in preheated oven for 15 minutes, stirring twice, until crumbs start to turn golden and crisp. Remove from oven and set aside to cool.

2 Meanwhile, gently squeeze salmon to remove excess moisture and place in a bowl. Add eggs, mayonnaise, lemon zest and juice, mustard, chives, dill, salt and pepper. Using a fork, mash salmon and mix gently. Add crumbs and mix well.

3 Scrape mixture into prepared loaf pan and pat with fork to even and smooth top. Bake in preheated oven for 1 to 1¼ hours or until top looks dry and loaf slowly springs back when lightly pressed.

4 Remove from oven and place on a wire rack. Set aside to firm up for 15 minutes. Loosen at the ends by pushing a thin knife between the loaf and the pan. Using the parchment sling, lift out loaf and transfer it to a cutting board. Slice and serve warm or allow to cool to room temperature.

TIPS

Lining the pan with a parchment sling allows you to lift out the loaf in one neat piece. Tear off a sheet of parchment wide enough to cover the bottom and long sides of the pan (about 8 inches/20 cm) and let it hang over the sides. Don't worry about lining the ends of the pan — the fishloaf isn't that sticky.

Oven temperatures vary quite a bit, which may affect the cooking time of this loaf. Look for signs of doneness: when you lightly press the loaf in the center, the indentation should slowly spring back. A slice cut from the middle while warm should hold together rather than breaking. Quick fix: If your slice of fishloaf isn't quite done, zap it in the microwave for 20 to 30 seconds. This works for fish burgers and fish cakes too.

For a smaller, faster fishloaf, halve the ingredients. Toast the bread crumbs for about 5 minutes and cook the fishloaf for about 30 minutes.

Substitute an equal quantity of tuna for the salmon.

Casseroles, Pies & Curries

Today's Tuna Noodle Casserole	130
Tuna Tetrazzini	132
Tuna à la King	134
Salmon Picadillo	135
Louisiana Clams and Corn	136
Crab Étouffé	137
Deviled Crab	138
Russian Salmon Pie	140
Clam Pie	142
Salmon and Leek Pot Pie	144
Shortcut Tuna Pot Pie	146
Jamaican Crab and Okra Curry	147
Coconut Tuna and Pea Curry	149

TODAY'S TUNA NOODLE CASSEROLE

MAKES 4 SERVINGS • Want to modernize your tuna noodle casserole? This is a step up from the vintage version; instead of canned soup it relies on béchamel sauce and fresh mushrooms. It still has, however, an old-fashioned comfort food vibe that your family will appreciate.

Food processor

8-inch (20 cm) square baking dish

UPTOWN CRUMB TOPPING

1 clove garlic

2 slices stale white bread (about 2½ oz/70 g), torn in pieces

½ cup (125 mL) freshly grated Parmesan cheese (1 oz/30 g; see Tips, page 131)

1 tbsp (15 mL) chopped parsley leaves

2 tbsp (30 mL) melted unsalted butter

CASSEROLE

1 cup (250 mL) trimmed green beans cut in thirds (4 oz/125 g)

6 oz (175 g) broad egg noodles

2 cups (500 mL) whole milk

¼ cup (60 mL) all-purpose flour

1 tsp (5 mL) fresh thyme leaves

1 tsp (5 mL) finely grated lemon zest

2 tbsp (30 mL) unsalted butter

1 leek, thinly sliced

1 stalk celery heart with leaves, chopped (see Tips, page 131)

2 tbsp (30 mL) chopped red bell pepper

1 cup (250 mL) sliced mushrooms (about 2 oz/60 g)

¼ tsp (1 mL) salt (approx.)

½ cup (125 mL) shredded Cheddar cheese (2 oz/60 g)

¼ cup (60 mL) sour cream

1 can (6 oz/170 g) tuna in water, drained and broken into chunks

Freshly ground black pepper

Preheat oven to 350°F (180°C)

1 UPTOWN CRUMB TOPPING: In food processor fitted with the metal blade, with the motor running, add garlic through the feed tube to chop. Scrape down the sides of the work bowl. Add bread and process it into coarse crumbs. Add Parmesan, parsley and butter. Pulse a few times until blended. Set aside

2 CASSEROLE: In a large pot of boiling salted water over medium heat, cook beans for 5 to 7 minutes, until tender-crisp. Using a mesh scoop, transfer to a sieve and rinse under cold running water. Drain and set aside.

3 Add noodles to pot and cook over medium heat for 10 to 12 minutes, until tender. Drain and set aside.

4 Meanwhile, in a large measuring cup, whisk together milk, flour, thyme and lemon zest.

5 In a saucepan over medium-low heat, melt butter. Add leek, celery, red pepper, mushrooms and salt. Cook, stirring occasionally, for 5 minutes, until vegetables are softened. Stir in milk mixture. Cook, stirring often, until thickened, about 2 to 3 minutes. Stir in cheese until melted. Stir in sour cream and remove from heat. Add tuna and reserved beans and noodles. Stir to blend and season to taste with pepper and additional salt, if necessary.

6 Scrape mixture into baking dish and scatter topping evenly over top. Bake in preheated oven for 30 minutes, until sauce is bubbly and topping is golden. Let casserole rest for 10 minutes before serving.

TIPS

The fine texture of dry grated Parmesan works well in this recipe. It makes crumb toppings crisper. You can substitute $\frac{1}{4}$ cup (60 mL) dry grated Parmesan for the freshly grated kind.

This makes enough topping for a 4-to-6-serving casserole in an 8-inch (20 cm) square baking dish. You can halve or double the recipe.

I prefer to use whole milk to give this sauce a creamier consistency.

To maintain more control over the final result, I always use unsalted butter in recipes. With salted butter, the amount of salt varies by brand. And salted butter contains more moisture, which can affect some recipes. Salt also masks rancidity.

Never discard celery leaves; they are wonderful herbs. The tender inner stalks of celery are called the heart. You can also tenderize an outer stalk by peeling it.

VARIATIONS

Substitute an equal quantity of broccoli florets or peas for the green beans.

Substitute an equal quantity of salmon, mackerel or clams for the tuna.

TUNA TETRAZZINI

MAKES 4 SERVINGS • This casserole was named in honor of the plump and powerful nineteenth-century opera diva Luisa Tetrazzini. It was a rich dish, originally made with chicken or turkey. This tuna version cuts the fat by replacing most of the cream with stock and cream cheese.

8-inch (20 cm) square baking dish

- 8 oz (250 g) spaghettini
- 1½ cups (375 mL) chicken stock
- ¼ cup (60 mL) all-purpose flour
- 2 tbsp (30 mL) unsalted butter, divided
- 1 tbsp (15 mL) extra virgin olive oil
- 1 onion, diced
- ¼ cup (60 mL) finely chopped red bell pepper
- 2 cloves garlic, minced
- 12 oz (375 g) button mushrooms, sliced (4½ cups/1.125 L)
- ½ tsp (2 mL) salt (approx.)
- ½ tsp (2 mL) freshly ground black pepper
- ¼ cup (60 mL) dry sherry
- 1 tbsp (15 mL) heavy or whipping (35%) cream
- 2 oz (60 g) cream cheese (about ¼ cup/60 mL)
- 4 oz (125 g) freshly grated Parmesan cheese (about 2 cups/500 mL), divided
- 1 can (6 oz/170 g) tuna in water, drained and broken into chunks
- ½ cup (125 mL) slivered almonds
- ½ cup (125 mL) panko bread crumbs (see Tips, page 133)
- 4 lemon wedges

Preheat oven to 350°F (180°C)

1 In a large pot of boiling salted water over medium heat, cook pasta for about 10 minutes, until just tender to the bite (al dente). Drain and set aside.

2 Meanwhile, in a large measuring cup, whisk together stock and flour. Set aside.

3 In a large skillet over medium heat, melt 1 tbsp (15 mL) butter with oil. Add onion and red pepper. Cook, stirring often, for 2 minutes, until softened. Stir in garlic for 20 seconds. Add mushrooms, salt and pepper. Cook for 5 minutes or until liquid from the mushrooms is released and evaporates. Stir in sherry. Cook, stirring occasionally, for 2 minutes.

4 Gradually stir in stock mixture. Reduce heat to low and simmer for 5 minutes, stirring often, until mixture thickens. Stir in cream and cream cheese. Add all but ¼ cup (60 mL) Parmesan and cook, stirring, until melted.

5 Remove pan from heat and stir in pasta and tuna. Add salt to taste, if necessary. Scrape into baking dish and sprinkle almonds evenly over top.

6 In a microwave-safe bowl, melt remaining 1 tbsp (15 mL) butter in a microwave oven on High for 30 seconds. Add panko bread crumbs and remaining Parmesan and mix well. Sprinkle mixture evenly over surface of casserole.

7 Bake in preheated oven for 30 minutes, until bubbly and topping is golden brown. Remove from oven and let stand for 10 to 15 minutes before serving. Serve with lemon wedges alongside to squeeze over top.

TIPS

Thank heavens for panko bread crumbs — they are light yet crunchy, and way better than standard dry crumbs for casserole toppings. Supermarkets stock panko, usually in the sushi section.

Letting a casserole stand for a few minutes before serving allows it to suck up any excess moisture and set, so you can serve neater portions. It also cools a bit, so you don't burn your tongue.

VARIATION

For a more substantial casserole, double the quantity of tuna.

Substitute salmon, mackerel or clams for the tuna.

TUNA À LA KING

MAKES 4 SERVINGS • In the beginning, there was chicken à la king. Not long after, seafood à la king appeared, featuring anything from tuna to lobster. During wartime, à la kings made with canned seafood became symbols of thrifty dining. Ladle this dish over puff pastry shells with little caps, known as vols-au-vent, or mate it with rice, noodles, toast or crêpes.

1½ cups (375 mL) chicken stock

¼ cup (60 mL) all-purpose flour

¼ tsp (1 mL) dried thyme

¼ tsp (1 mL) freshly ground white pepper

1 tbsp (15 mL) unsalted butter

1 tbsp (15 mL) vegetable oil

2½ cups (625 mL) chopped button mushrooms (about 8 oz/250 g)

1 small onion, diced

1 carrot, chopped

½ tsp (2 mL) salt (approx.)

¼ cup (60 mL) dry white wine, optional

½ cup (125 mL) half-and-half (10%) cream

1 large egg yolk

1 can (6 oz/170 g) tuna in water, drained and broken into large chunks

¼ cup (60 mL) pimientos, drained and chopped

1 tbsp (15 mL) chopped parsley leaves

Sweet paprika

4 lemon wedges

1 In a large measuring cup, whisk together stock, flour, thyme and pepper.

2 In a large saucepan over medium heat, melt butter with oil. Add mushrooms, onion, carrot and salt and cook, stirring, for 10 minutes, until mushrooms release their liquid and carrot softens. Stir in wine, if using, and cook for 1 minute. Gradually stir in stock mixture. When mixture comes to a simmer, reduce heat to low and simmer for 5 minutes, until thickened. Stir in cream.

3 In a small bowl, stir together egg yolk and a small ladleful of the warm cream mixture. Return to pan, stir to blend for a few seconds, then remove from heat. Do not allow it to boil.

4 Gently stir in tuna, pimientos and parsley. Add salt to taste, if necessary.

5 Sprinkle paprika over top and serve immediately, with lemon wedges alongside to squeeze over.

Substitute an equal quantity of salmon, mackerel or crab for the tuna.

SALMON PICADILLO

MAKES 4 SERVINGS • Piquant Latin American picadillo, usually made with ground beef, is an economical and enjoyable meal. Although seafood may seem like an odd substitute, the flavor combos work well. The slightly sweet, slightly sour sauce complements salmon. Serve it over rice or couscous.

- 1 tbsp (15 mL) extra virgin olive oil
- 4 large green onions (white and light green parts), sliced
- 2 cloves garlic, minced
- 1 stalk celery heart with leaves, chopped
- 1 cup (250 mL) prepared tomato sauce
- ¼ cup (60 mL) water
- 1 tbsp white vinegar
- 2 plum tomatoes, coarsely chopped
- 1 apple, skin on, cored and chopped
- ¼ cup (60 mL) raisins
- ¼ cup (60 mL) sliced pimiento-stuffed green olives (4 large)
- 1 tsp (5 mL) granulated sugar
- ½ tsp (2 mL) ground cumin
- ¼ tsp (1 mL) ground cinnamon
- ¼ tsp (1 mL) salt (approx.)
- ¼ tsp (1 mL) freshly ground black pepper
- 1 can (7½ oz/213 g) salmon, drained, deboned and broken into chunks
- 3 tbsp (45 mL) slivered almonds, toasted (see Tips, below)

1 In a skillet, heat oil over medium heat until shimmery. Add green onions, garlic and celery and cook, stirring often, for 1 to 2 minutes, until vegetables start to turn golden. Stir in tomato sauce, water, vinegar, tomatoes, apple, raisins, olives, sugar, cumin, cinnamon, salt and pepper and bring to a simmer.

2 Reduce heat to medium-low, cover and simmer for 15 minutes, stirring occasionally. (If necessary to maintain a simmer, reduce heat to low.) Remove from heat and stir in salmon. Add salt to taste, if necessary.

3 Sprinkle almonds evenly over top and serve immediately.

TIPS

I prefer to use the tender inner stalks of celery known as the heart. You can, however, tenderize an outside stalk by peeling it.

Toast almonds in a dry skillet over medium heat, shaking pan often, for about 3 minutes, until golden and fragrant.

Substitute an equal quantity of tuna for the salmon.

CASSEROLES, PIES & CURRIES

LOUISIANA CLAMS AND CORN

MAKES 6 SERVINGS • I love to sink my teeth into maque choux, a Louisiana dish chockfull of corn, peppers, tomato and bacon. It is often served as a side dish, but adding clams (or other seafood) makes it a hearty and colorful meal. Spoon it over a bed of rice.

4 slices bacon, thinly sliced crosswise

1 tbsp (15 mL) unsalted butter

4 cloves garlic, minced

2 shallots, finely diced

1 red bell pepper, cut in small dice

1 jalapeño pepper, seeded and cut in small dice

½ tsp (2 mL) salt (approx.)

⅛ tsp (0.5 mL) freshly ground black pepper

1 tsp (5 mL) Cajun seasoning

1½ cups (375 mL) trimmed, thinly sliced okra (6 oz/175 g)

2¼ cups (550 mL) corn kernels (about 12 oz/375 g)

1 plum tomato, peeled and diced

6 green onions (white and light green parts), thinly sliced

1 can (5 oz/142 g) surf or meaty clams, rinsed, drained and chopped

1 In a 12-inch (30 cm) skillet over medium heat, cook bacon for about 5 minutes, until browned and crisp. Using a slotted spoon, transfer to a plate lined with paper towels.

2 Drain all but 1 tbsp (15 mL) drippings from skillet. Over medium heat, stir in butter until it melts. Add garlic, shallots, red pepper, jalapeño, salt, pepper and Cajun seasoning. Cook, stirring occasionally, for about 3 minutes, until vegetables soften. Increase heat to medium-high. Add okra and cook for 2 minutes, stirring occasionally. Add corn and cook for 2 to 3 minutes, until okra is tender-crisp and corn is heated through.

3 Remove skillet from heat. Stir in tomato, onions, clams and bacon. Add salt to taste, if necessary. Serve immediately.

TIP

If using thawed frozen okra instead of fresh pods, add it to the pan along with the corn.

Substitute an equal quantity of tuna, salmon, mackerel or crab for the clams.

CASSEROLES, PIES & CURRIES

CRAB ÉTOUFFÉ

MAKES 4 SMALL SERVINGS • Here's more Louisiana comfort food. It looks best with large lump crabmeat but you can enjoy it with less expensive claw or small chunk crab. Serve this saucy dish over rice.

2 tsp (10 mL) fresh thyme leaves

1 tsp (5 mL) sweet paprika

½ tsp (2 mL) freshly ground black pepper

¼ tsp (1 mL) salt (approx.)

2 tbsp (30 mL) unsalted butter

1½ cups (375 mL) canned crabmeat (8 oz/250 g), rinsed and drained

2 tbsp (30 mL) vegetable oil

2 tbsp (30 mL) all-purpose flour

1 small onion, diced

1 stalk celery, cut in ¼-inch (0.5 cm) dice

½ small green bell pepper, cut in ¼-inch (0.5 cm) dice

2 cloves garlic, minced

1 cup (250 mL) chicken or vegetable stock

1 bay leaf

2 tbsp (30 mL) heavy or whipping (35%) cream

Hot pepper sauce

2 tbsp (30 mL) chopped parsley leaves

1 In a small bowl, stir together thyme, paprika, pepper and salt.

2 In a saucepan over medium-low heat, melt butter. Add crab and half the spice mixture. Cook for 2 minutes, stirring gently a couple of times. Transfer to a bowl, cover and set aside.

3 Add oil to pan and place over medium heat until shimmery. Stir in flour. Cook, stirring, for 3 to 5 minutes, until mixture is brown and has a nutty scent. Add onion, celery and green pepper. Cook, stirring, for about 2 minutes, until vegetables soften. Stir in garlic and remaining spice mixture for 1 minute. Stir in stock and add bay leaf. When mixture comes to a simmer, reduce heat to low. Cover and simmer for 10 minutes, until vegetables are tender.

4 Discard bay leaf. Stir in cream and crab mixture and simmer for 2 minutes. Add salt to taste, if necessary. Season liberally with hot pepper sauce.

5 Serve immediately, garnished with parsley.

Substitute an equal quantity of tuna, salmon or clams for the crab. If substituting flaky fish such as tuna or salmon, stir it in at the end.

DEVILED CRAB

> **MAKES 4 SMALL SERVINGS** • Hot pepper sauce, mustard and crumbs make these little crab casseroles devilishly good. Serve them as an appetizer course or as brunch or luncheon treats with green salad.

Food processor
Four ¾-cup (175 mL) ramekins

1 slice stale white bread (about 1¼ oz/35 g)

3 tbsp (45 mL) unsalted butter, divided

1 tbsp (15 mL) chopped parsley leaves

1 cup (250 mL) whole milk (see Tips, page 139)

2 tbsp (30 mL) all-purpose flour

1 tbsp (15 mL) dry sherry

1 tsp (5 mL) Dijon mustard

¼ tsp (1 mL) salt (approx.)

⅛ tsp (0.5 mL) freshly ground white pepper

¼ cup (60 mL) chopped white onion

¼ cup (60 mL) chopped green bell pepper

¼ cup (60 mL) chopped celery heart (see Tips, page 139)

1 clove garlic, minced

1½ cups (375 mL) canned crabmeat (8 oz/250 g), rinsed and drained (see Tips, page 139)

1 tbsp (15 mL) hot pepper sauce

Preheat oven to 350°F (180°C)

1 In food processor fitted with the metal blade, process bread into fine crumbs (you should have about ¾ cup/175 mL). In a medium bowl, melt 1 tbsp (15 mL) butter in a microwave oven on High for 20 to 30 seconds. Stir in bread crumbs and parsley. Set aside.

2 In a large measuring cup, whisk together milk, flour, sherry, mustard, salt and pepper.

3 In a saucepan over medium-low heat, melt remaining 2 tbsp (30 mL) butter. Add onion, green pepper, celery and garlic. Cook, stirring often, for about 5 minutes, until vegetables soften.

4 Gradually add milk mixture, stirring constantly. Cook, stirring often, for 3 to 5 minutes, until mixture thickens. Stir in crab and heat for 1 minute. Add hot pepper sauce. Add salt to taste, if necessary.

5 Divide mixture evenly among ramekins. Sprinkle crumb mixture over top. Place ramekins on a rimmed baking sheet and bake in preheated oven for 30 minutes, until sauce is bubbly and topping is golden. Serve immediately.

TIPS

Keep the sauce suitably creamy by using whole milk.

Use one of the tender inner stalks of celery, known as the heart.

Go upscale with a 1-pound (454 g) container of white lump crabmeat or keep costs down by buying two less expensive 4¼-oz (120 g) shelf-stable cans of claw or flaked crab.

Substitute an equal quantity of tuna, salmon or mackerel for the crab.

RUSSIAN SALMON PIE

> **MAKES 6 SERVINGS** • Coulibiac is the fancy name for this salmon and rice pie. You don't have to wait for a special occasion to prepare it: coulibiac makes an appealing family meal. Originating in Russia as *kulebyaka*, this pie was popularized by French chefs in the nineteenth century.

Rimmed baking sheet, lined with parchment

FILLING

1/3 cup (75 mL) long-grain white rice, rinsed

2/3 cup (150 mL) water

3/4 tsp (3 mL) salt (approx.), divided

1 tbsp (15 mL) vegetable oil

3 cups (750 mL) sliced button or cremini mushrooms (8 oz/250 g; see Tips, page 141)

1 cup (250 mL) thinly sliced leek (about 1/2)

2 cans (each 7 1/2 oz/213 g) salmon, drained, deboned and broken into chunks

3 large eggs, hard-cooked and coarsely chopped

1/4 cup (60 mL) chopped parsley leaves

1 tbsp (15 mL) chopped fresh dill fronds

1/4 tsp (1 mL) freshly ground black pepper

PASTRY

1 large egg

1 tbsp (15 mL) cold water

1 lb (500 g) puff pastry (approx.), thawed, at room temperature (see Tips, page 141)

Flour for dusting

SAUCE (OPTIONAL)

1 cup (250 mL) sour cream

1 tbsp (15 mL) vodka

1 tbsp (15 mL) chopped chives

Salt

1 tbsp (15 mL) black or red lumpfish caviar (roe)

Preheat oven to 400°F (200°C)

1 FILLING: In a small saucepan over high heat, bring rice, water and 1/8 tsp (0.5 mL) salt to a boil. Reduce heat to low, cover and simmer for about 15 minutes, until water is absorbed and rice is tender. Fluff with a fork and set aside to cool to room temperature.

2 In a skillet (preferably nonstick), heat oil over medium heat until shimmery. Add mushrooms, leek and 1/8 tsp (0.5 mL) salt. Cook, stirring often, for about 5 minutes, until liquid from mushrooms is released and evaporates. Set aside and cool to room temperature.

3 Add rice, salmon, eggs, parsley, dill, 1/2 tsp (2 mL) salt and pepper to mushrooms. Mix gently with a fork. Add salt to taste, if necessary.

4 PASTRY: In a small bowl, whisk together egg and water.

5 Cut pastry into 2 pieces, one slightly larger. On a lightly floured surface, roll the larger piece into a rectangle 14 by 10 inches (35 by 25 cm). Place on prepared baking sheet and brush with egg wash. Spread filling over pastry, leaving a 1-inch (2.5 cm) border. Roll remaining pastry into a rectangle 12 by 8 inches (30 by 20 cm). Place over filling. Fold edges of bottom pastry up to cover top pastry. Using a fork, press along the border to seal. Brush top with egg wash (you will have some left over).

6 Bake in preheated oven for 25 to 30 minutes, until pie is golden brown. Let rest for 5 minutes before serving.

7 SAUCE (IF USING): In a small serving bowl, stir together sour cream, vodka, chives and salt to taste. Just before serving, rinse the caviar and drain well. Scatter over the sour cream. Serve sauce alongside slices of pie.

TIPS

Puff pastry packages vary in size. If available, use a 14 ounce (400 g) package, which is just the right amount for this recipe.

Many cooks prepare the filling in layers, but I like to mix the salmon with the rice to keep it moist.

No need to fuss with mushroom brushes. You can rinse dirt off mushrooms; just don't let them soak. They are absorbent, but liquid is released in the hot pan.

VARIATIONS

If you prefer, serve plain sour cream or hollandaise sauce instead of the vodka sauce.

Instead of making a traditional coulibiac, substitute tuna or mackerel for the salmon.

CASSEROLES, PIES & CURRIES

CLAM PIE

MAKES 6 SERVINGS • Carb alert! Clam pie is like eating clam chowder in pastry, and it's addictively delicious. Like many vintage seafood recipes, clam pie dates back to the 1890s. Culinary historians say it was a thrifty meal enthusiastically and frequently consumed by working-class families, particularly in East Hampton, New York, and among the Acadians. While they used fresh clams, this version is equally appealing but far less work.

9- or 10-inch (23 or 25 cm) deep-dish pie plate

Rimmed baking sheet

4 slices bacon, chopped

1 lb (500 g) potatoes (4), peeled and cut in ¼-inch (0.5 cm) dice (see Tips, page 143)

1 carrot (about 2 oz/60 g), cut in ¼-inch (0.5 cm) dice

1 onion, diced

1 clove garlic, minced

½ tsp (2 mL) salt (approx.)

1 bottle (8 oz/240 mL) clam juice (see Tips, page 143)

1 tsp (5 mL) finely grated lemon zest

2 tsp (10 mL) fresh thyme leaves

½ tsp (2 mL) poultry seasoning (see Tips, page 143)

¼ tsp (1 mL) freshly ground black pepper

¾ cup (175 mL) heavy or whipping (35%) cream

2 tbsp (30 mL) all-purpose flour

1 can (5 oz/142 g) surf or meaty clams, drained and coarsely chopped

Pastry for a double-crust pie

Preheat oven to 400°F (200°C), placing rack in lowest position (see Tips, page 143)

1 In a large saucepan over medium heat, cook bacon for about 5 minutes, until browned and crisp. Using a slotted spoon, transfer to a plate lined with paper towels to drain.

2 Add potatoes, carrot, onion, garlic and salt to the drippings and cook, stirring often, for about 5 minutes, until softened. Add clam juice, lemon zest, thyme, poultry seasoning and pepper. Reduce heat to low, cover and cook for 10 minutes, until vegetables are almost tender.

3 In a measuring cup, whisk together cream and flour. Gradually stir into clam mixture and bring to a simmer. Cook for 1 to 2 minutes, until thickened. Stir in clams and reserved bacon. Remove pan from heat and set aside to cool for 30 minutes, stirring occasionally to disperse the heat. Add salt to taste, if necessary.

4 Press dough for bottom crust into pie plate. Add cooled filling. Place top crust over filling, trimming and crimping the edges. Cut 8 long slits in a spoke pattern on top. Place pie on baking sheet and bake in preheated oven for 30 minutes, until crust is golden. Reduce oven temperature to 350°F (180°C), rotate baking sheet and bake for 30 minutes more, until filling is bubbly and crust is golden brown.

5 Transfer to a wire rack and let cool for 15 to 30 minutes. Serve warm or at room temperature.

TIPS

I use yellow-fleshed potatoes in this pie, as they are somewhat creamy but still hold their shape. Try to go by weight, as the amount will affect the consistency of the filling.

Placing the oven rack in the lowest position helps to keep the bottom crust crispy and prevents the top crust from browning too quickly.

Poultry seasoning is a spice blend sold in supermarkets.

Don't substitute the liquid from canned clams for bottled clam juice. The former usually contains additives.

You need meaty clams for this pie. Baby clams are too delicate.

If desired, buy pre-chopped clams.

VARIATION

If you don't want to make a double-crust pie, put the filling in a casserole dish, cover the top with pastry dough and reduce the baking time by about 15 minutes, or bake until the filling is bubbly and the crust is golden brown.

SALMON AND LEEK POT PIE

MAKES 6 SERVINGS • Serve up some nostalgia with this old-school pie. The thick, mild-mannered leek and parsley sauce is an appealing partner for flavorful salmon.

Rimmed baking sheet
9-inch (23 cm) pie plate

1 cup (250 mL) whole milk (see Tip, below)
½ cup (125 mL) chicken stock
¼ cup (60 mL) all-purpose flour
2 tbsp (30 mL) unsalted butter
2 leeks (white and light green parts), thinly sliced
½ tsp (2 mL) salt (approx.)
2 cloves garlic, minced
¼ cup (60 mL) dry white wine
2 cans (each 7½ oz/213 g) salmon, drained, deboned and broken into chunks
1 small roasted red pepper, diced
¼ cup (60 mL) chopped parsley leaves
1 tsp (5 mL) finely grated lemon zest
⅛ tsp (0.5 mL) freshly ground white pepper
Pastry for a single-crust pie

Preheat oven to 375°F (190°C)

1 In a bowl, whisk together milk, stock and flour.

2 In a saucepan over medium heat, melt butter. Add leeks and salt. Cook, stirring often, for about 5 minutes, until leeks soften and turn golden. Stir in garlic for 30 seconds. Stir in wine for 30 to 60 seconds, until it has almost evaporated. Stir in milk mixture and bring to a boil. Reduce heat to medium-low and simmer for 3 to 5 minutes, until leeks are tender and sauce is very thick. Remove from heat.

3 Stir in salmon, roasted red pepper, parsley, lemon zest and ground pepper. Add salt to taste, if necessary.

4 Scrape mixture into pie plate. Slash a few vents in the pastry and place it over filling. Press edges onto rim of pie plate. Place pie on baking sheet.

5 Bake in preheated oven for about 30 minutes, until pastry is golden brown and filling is bubbly. Let pie rest for 10 minutes before serving.

TIP
I use whole milk to make the sauce creamier.

Substitute an equal quantity of tuna, mackerel or clams for the salmon.

SHORTCUT TUNA POT PIE

MAKES 9 SMALL SERVINGS • Add a store-bought biscuit topping to creamed tuna and vegetables, and presto, you've got a humble but appealing pot pie. My family makes short work of this pie once it hits the table.

8-inch (20 cm) square baking dish

- 2 tbsp (30 mL) unsalted butter
- 1 small onion, chopped
- ½ red bell pepper, chopped
- 1 stalk celery, chopped (see Tips, below)
- ¼ cup (60 mL) all-purpose flour
- 1 cup (250 mL) chicken stock
- 1 cup (250 mL) whole milk
- ½ cup (125 mL) green peas, thawed if frozen
- ½ cup (125 mL) corn kernels, thawed if frozen
- 2 tbsp (30 mL) chopped parsley leaves
- 1 tsp (5 mL) chopped fresh dill fronds
- ½ tsp (2 mL) mustard powder
- 1 tbsp (15 mL) freshly squeezed lemon juice
- 1 can (6 oz/170 g) tuna in water, drained and broken into chunks
- 1 tube (12 oz/340 g) refrigerated "country biscuit" dough

Preheat oven to 375°F (190°C)

1 In a skillet over medium heat, melt butter. Add onion, red pepper and celery and cook, stirring often, for 5 minutes, until vegetables soften. Stir in flour and cook for 1 minute. Gradually whisk in stock, then milk. When mixture comes to a simmer, stir in peas, corn, parsley, dill and mustard. Reduce heat to medium-low. Simmer, stirring often, for about 10 minutes, until mixture is thickened and vegetables are tender. Stir in lemon juice, then tuna.

2 Scrape mixture into baking dish and lay 9 dough rounds on top. (You will have one left over; see Tips, below). Bake in preheated oven for about 15 minutes, until biscuits are golden and filling is bubbling at the edges. Let rest for 5 minutes before serving.

TIPS

Place the leftover biscuit dough on a greased square of foil and bake it alongside.

I prefer to use the tender inner stalks of celery known as the heart. You can, however, tenderize an outside stalk by peeling it.

Substitute salmon, mackerel or clams for the tuna.

JAMAICAN CRAB AND OKRA CURRY

> **MAKES 4 SMALL SERVINGS** • Give okra a chance. When properly cooked, this unfairly maligned vegetable is tender-crisp and delightfully peppery, not limp and slimy. Okra adds tasty texture to this Caribbean-style curry. Serve it over rice.

- 2 tbsp (30 mL) extra virgin olive oil
- 2 tbsp (30 mL) curry powder
- 1 onion, diced
- 1 large clove garlic, minced
- ⅓ cup (75 mL) chopped red bell pepper
- ½ tsp (2 mL) hot pepper flakes
- ½ tsp (2 mL) salt (approx.)
- ¼ tsp (1 mL) freshly ground black pepper
- 3 tbsp (45 mL) tomato paste
- 1 cup (250 mL) chicken or vegetable stock, divided
- 1 cup (250 mL) trimmed, sliced (¼ inch/0.5 cm) okra (about 4 oz/125 g)
- 1 green onion, trimmed and sliced
- 1¼ cups (300 mL) canned crabmeat, rinsed and drained (6 oz/175 g) (see Tips, below)
- ½ cup (125 mL) water, optional

1 In a saucepan, heat oil over medium heat until shimmery. Add curry powder and cook, stirring constantly, for 30 to 60 seconds, until dark brown but not burned. Add onion, garlic, red pepper, hot pepper flakes, salt and pepper. Cook, stirring constantly, for 2 to 3 minutes. Stir in tomato paste and ½ cup (125 mL) stock. Cook, stirring often, for 3 minutes.

2 Stir in remaining stock along with okra and green onion. Reduce the heat to medium-low, cover and cook for about 3 minutes, until okra is tender-crisp. Stir in crab and cook for 1 minute, until heated through. If necessary, add some or all of the water to adjust the consistency. (The sauce should be like thick gravy.) Adjust salt to taste and serve immediately.

TIPS

The crab should be chunky rather than flaky. For best results, buy pasteurized lump crabmeat. You can use the remainder of a pound (500 g) container in other dishes.

Use thawed frozen okra if you can't find fresh. Add it with the crab and cook just until it's heated through.

VARIATIONS

Replace the hot pepper flakes with some Scotch bonnet or habanero pepper. These are among the hottest peppers in the world, so start with a ¼-inch (0.5 cm) slice, minced.

COCONUT TUNA AND PEA CURRY

MAKES 4 SMALL SERVINGS • This is not an authentic curry and the heat is an afterthought, but the creamy coconut sauce makes it comfort food for young and old. It is good, fast food for a light dinner. Serve it over rice or toast.

- 1 tbsp (15 mL) vegetable oil
- 1 small onion, diced
- 1 clove garlic, minced
- 2 tsp (10 mL) curry powder
- 1 can (14 oz/398 mL) coconut milk (see Tip, below)
- 3 tbsp (45 mL) chopped cilantro leaves, divided
- ½ tsp (2 mL) salt (approx.)
- 1 bay leaf
- 1 cup (250 mL) green peas, thawed if frozen
- 1 can (6 oz/170 g) tuna in water, drained and broken into chunks
- 1 tbsp (15 mL) freshly squeezed lime juice
- Hot pepper sauce

1 In a saucepan, heat oil over medium heat until shimmery. Add onion and cook, stirring often, for 3 to 5 minutes, until it softens and starts to turn golden. Add garlic and cook, stirring, for 20 seconds. Stir in curry powder. Add coconut milk, 2 tbsp (30 mL) cilantro, salt and bay leaf. Bring to a simmer. Reduce heat to medium-low and simmer for 5 minutes, until onion is soft and the sauce thickens. Remove and discard bay leaf.

2 Add peas and tuna and stir well. Simmer for 2 minutes, until heated through. Stir in lime juice. Add salt to taste, if necessary, and season to taste with hot pepper sauce.

3 Garnish with remaining cilantro and serve immediately.

TIP
Use "lite" coconut milk if you prefer.

Substitute an equal quantity of salmon, mackerel or crab for the tuna.

Pasta, Rice & Grains

Sicilian-Style Sardine Pasta	152
Pasta with Tuna, Beans, Sage and Olives	155
Tuna and Olive Rotini	156
Vintage Tuna Mac and Cheese	157
Tuna Pantry Pasta	158
Tortellini Toss-Up	160
Tuna Fettuccine Alfredo	161
The Ziti Caper	162
Pasta with Spicy Salmon and Rapini	163
Jumbo Shells Stuffed with Salmon, Ricotta and Zucchini	164
Orzo with Salmon, Asparagus and Smoked Mozzarella	166
Caesar Spaghettini	167
Penne with Anchovied Broccolini	168
Spanish Noodles	169
Spaghetti with Clam Sauce Two Ways	170
Clam Carbonara	173
Fishballs in White Wine Tomato Basil Sauce	174
Lemony Salmon and Asparagus Risotto	176
Tuna and Spinach Risotto	178
Easy Ham and Clam Jambalaya	179
Portuguese Rice with Clams	180
Moroccan-Style Salmon Quinoa	181
Citrus Quinoa with Crab and Cress	182

SICILIAN-STYLE SARDINE PASTA

> **MAKES 4 SMALL SERVINGS** • This dish may sound strange but it tastes good. *Pasta con le sarde* is a Sicilian classic starring sardines, fennel and bucatini. Although many cooks will disagree, I go by the nothing-is-sacred philosophy of cooking. So my knock-off calls for canned sardines, omits the Arab-influenced raisins and pine nuts, and gussies up the crumb topping.

Food processor
Rimmed baking sheet

1 bulb fennel

2 slices stale white bread (about 2½ oz/70 g)

½ cup + 1 tbsp (140 mL) extra virgin olive oil, divided

1 large clove garlic, minced

1 onion, diced

½ tsp (2 mL) salt (approx.)

½ cup (125 mL) dry white wine

¼ tsp (1 mL) saffron threads, crumbled, optional

12 oz (375 g) bucatini (see Tips, page 153)

2 tins (each 4 oz/120 g) boneless, skinless sardines in oil, drained

Preheat oven or toaster oven to 300°F (150°C) (see Tips, page 153)

1 Slice off the top of the fennel with the tough stalks. Remove the tender leafy fronds, chop and set aside (you should have 2 to 4 tbsp/30 to 60 mL). Discard stalks. Cut a thin slice off the base of the bulb and discard. Cut bulb in half lengthwise. Cut out and discard the triangular core from each half. Discard any browned outer layers. Cut each half into thin slivers, then crosswise to obtain a ⅛- to ¼-inch (3 to 5 mm) dice (you should have about 2½ cups/625 mL).

2 In food processor fitted with the metal blade, process bread into fine crumbs (you should have about 1½ cups/375 mL). Transfer to baking sheet and toast in preheated oven for 5 to 10 minutes, stirring twice, until golden brown. Remove from oven and let cool to room temperature. When cool, drizzle with 1 tbsp (15 mL) olive oil. Sprinkle garlic, fennel fronds and salt to taste over top. Blend with a fork and set aside.

3 Bring a large pot of salted water to a boil over high heat.

4 Meanwhile, in a skillet, heat remaining ½ cup (125 mL) oil over medium heat until shimmery. Add diced fennel, onion and salt. Cook, stirring occasionally, for 10 minutes, until fennel is tender and golden brown. Add wine and saffron, if using. Simmer for 1 minute. Remove from heat and set aside.

5 Add bucatini to the boiling water and cook over medium heat for about 15 minutes, until tender to the bite (al dente). Scoop out about ½ cup (125 mL) cooking water and set aside. Drain pasta.

6 In a large warmed serving bowl, toss bucatini with fennel mixture. If pasta seems dry or difficult to toss evenly, add enough reserved cooking water to moisten and loosen it. Add the sardines and toss gently.

7 Sprinkle crumb mixture over top. Serve immediately.

TIPS

When making bread crumbs for this recipe, I like to use whole wheat and/or rye bread for full flavor.

If you prefer, toast the crumbs in your toaster oven rather than in the oven (Step 2). Place them on the miniature baking sheet that comes with the oven.

Bucatini are long pasta straws. They are sometimes called perciatelli.

VARIATION

You can use regular sardines, but they are more tender and likelier to fall apart than the boneless, skinless fillets.

Substitute an equal quantity of mackerel for the sardines.

COOKING PASTA

Traditional wisdom suggests that pasta should be cooked at a rolling boil, which some cooks translate to mean constant high heat. However, medium heat is fine. The water will still maintain a lively boil and the cook will save a bit on energy costs. Medium heat is also better for pots — if you read the fine print in some stainless steel cookware brochures, high heat is not recommended for longest life.

Interestingly, you don't actually need to boil pasta at all. Not to be too scientific, but this is related to the fact that starches start to absorb water at well below the boiling point. You can bring water to a boil, toss in the pasta, cover the pot, turn off the heat and let it sit. The timing is tricky, however, and the texture of the cooked pasta seems to end up a bit uneven. So I'll stick to my old-fashioned method of boiling on medium heat.

PASTA WITH TUNA, BEANS, SAGE AND OLIVES

MAKES 4 TO 6 SERVINGS • I get cravings for this hearty pasta, which is packed with wholesome nourishment.

12 oz (375 g) whole wheat cavatappi (see Tips, below)	2 cups (500 mL) cherry tomatoes, quartered
½ cup (125 mL) lightly packed sage leaves, divided	1 cup (250 mL) black olives, pitted and coarsely chopped
2 tbsp (30 mL) extra virgin olive oil	1 can (6 oz/170 g) tuna in water, drained and broken into chunks
2 cloves garlic, minced	¼ tsp (1 mL) salt (approx.)
1 can (14 to 19 oz/398 to 540 mL) cannellini (white kidney) beans, rinsed and drained (see Tips, below)	¼ tsp (1 mL) freshly ground black pepper

1 In a large pot of boiling salted water, cook pasta over medium heat for about 10 minutes, until tender to the bite (al dente). Scoop out about ½ cup (125 mL) cooking water and set aside. Drain pasta.

2 Meanwhile, finely chop 2 of the sage leaves and set aside. Cut remainder into thin slivers. Set aside separately.

3 In a skillet, heat oil over medium heat until shimmery. Stir in garlic for 20 seconds. Stir in slivered sage and beans. Heat for 1 minute. Remove from heat and add tomatoes and olives.

4 In a large warmed bowl, toss together pasta, tuna, bean mixture, salt and pepper. If pasta seems dry or difficult to toss evenly, add enough reserved cooking water to moisten and loosen it. Add salt to taste, if necessary. Sprinkle with chopped sage and serve immediately.

TIPS

Cavatappi looks like penne twisted into a spiral. It is sometimes labeled "scoobi doo." You can substitute whole wheat macaroni, penne or rotini.

I prefer to use the 19 ounce (540 mL) can of beans.

VARIATIONS

Use any type of beans in your cupboard.

Substitute an equal quantity of salmon or mackerel for the tuna.

TUNA AND OLIVE ROTINI

MAKES 4 SERVINGS • A bit of tuna can go a long way in pasta. This rotini is both tasty and pretty, thanks to the corkscrew noodles, green olives and red pepper.

12 oz (375 g) rotini

2 cans (each 3 oz/85 g) tuna in olive oil, with oil

1 cup (250 mL) sliced pitted green olives (20 large)

1 small red bell pepper, slivered

1 large clove garlic, minced

2 tbsp (30 mL) extra virgin olive oil

½ tsp (2 mL) salt (approx.)

¼ tsp (1 mL) freshly ground black pepper

½ cup (125 mL) parsley leaves, coarsely chopped

1 In a large pot of boiling salted water, cook rotini over medium heat for about 12 minutes, until tender to the bite (al dente). Scoop out about ½ cup (125 mL) cooking water and set aside. Drain pasta.

2 Meanwhile, in a large warmed serving bowl, stir together tuna, with oil, olives, red pepper, garlic, extra virgin olive oil, salt and pepper. Add rotini. If the pasta seems dry or clumpy, add enough reserved cooking water to moisten and loosen it. Add salt to taste, if necessary.

3 Scatter parsley over top and serve immediately.

TIP
Save some of the starchy cooking water in case your pasta seems dry or difficult to toss evenly. Add the water in stages.

VARIATION
If the seafood you are using is not packed in olive oil, add an extra 2 tbsp (30 mL) extra virgin olive oil to this dish.

Substitute an equal quantity of salmon or sardines for the tuna.

VINTAGE TUNA MAC AND CHEESE

MAKES 4 TO 6 SERVINGS • This simple old-school comfort food dish, its source forgotten in the mists of time, makes me feel like a kid when I eat it. It is quickly prepared on the stovetop and, yes, it calls for a can of condensed soup.

12 oz (375 g) elbow macaroni (about 3 cups/750 mL)	3 cups (750 mL) shredded sharp (old) Cheddar cheese (12 oz/375 g)
2 tbsp (30 mL) unsalted butter	1 can (6 oz/170 g) tuna in water, drained and broken into chunks
1 small onion, chopped	
1 stalk celery, chopped	4 canned plum tomatoes, drained and coarsely chopped
1 can (10 oz/284 mL) condensed cream of mushroom soup	Salt and freshly ground black pepper
1 cup (250 mL) milk (see Tip, below)	

1 In a large pot of boiling salted water, cook macaroni over medium heat for about 12 minutes, until tender to the bite (al dente). Drain.

2 Meanwhile, in a large saucepan, melt butter over medium-low heat. Add onion and celery and cook, stirring often, for 5 minutes, until vegetables soften. Add soup and milk and stir well to smooth out lumps. After mixture comes to a simmer, cook, stirring often, for 5 minutes. Stir in cheese until melted. Stir in tuna and tomatoes. Remove from heat.

3 Stir in macaroni and season to taste with salt and pepper. Serve immediately.

TIP

I use whole milk to make the sauce creamy.

Substitute an equal quantity of salmon or mackerel for the tuna.

PASTA, RICE & GRAINS

TUNA PANTRY PASTA

MAKES 4 SERVINGS • This simple, any day dinner dish would be right at home on a sunny Mediterranean table. You can throw it together in no time with pantry ingredients.

- 12 oz (375 g) penne
- 3 cans (each 3 oz/85 g) solid tuna in olive oil
- 1 tsp (5 mL) freshly squeezed lemon juice
- 4 cloves garlic, pressed or minced
- ½ tsp (2 mL) finely grated lemon zest
- ¼ tsp (1 mL) hot pepper flakes
- 1½ cups (375 mL) fire-roasted diced tomatoes
- 1 tsp (5 mL) kosher salt (approx.)
- ¼ cup (60 mL) thinly sliced basil leaves
- Freshly ground black pepper
- 1 tbsp (15 mL) chopped parsley

1 In large pan of boiling, salted water, cook penne 12 minutes or according to package directions, until tender to the bite (al dente).

2 Meanwhile, drain tuna in fine-mesh sieve set over medium measuring cup. Separate tuna into bite-sized chunks. Toss with lemon juice.

3 Add ¼ cup (60 mL) oil from tuna to medium pan. (Reserve any remaining oil for other uses.) Add garlic, zest and hot pepper flakes. Stir on medium heat 1 minute, or until fragrant and sizzling. (Do not brown.) Stir in tomatoes and 1 tsp (5 mL) salt. When liquid comes to boil, reduce heat to medium-low. Simmer, stirring often, 5 minutes, or until slightly thickened. Remove from heat.

4 Drain pasta. Stir basil and pasta into sauce. Adjust salt. Gently stir in tuna. Before serving, grind pepper over top and garnish with parsley.

TIPS

You can use any type of pasta. The sauce combines best with short pastas, including bows and shells.

If you don't have tuna in olive oil, drain it. Use extra virgin olive oil instead of the tuna oil.

For the finest mince, push the garlic through a press.

Most supermarkets sell fire-roasted diced tomatoes. You may substitute a 14 oz (398 mL) can of standard diced tomatoes.

Instead of tuna, use canned salmon, clams, crab or sardines. If using sardines, arrange whole sardines on top of the pasta with sauce.

TORTELLINI TOSS-UP

MAKES 4 SERVINGS • This easy pasta is halfway between homemade and store-bought, and all-the-way delicious.

2 cans (each 3 oz/85 g) tuna in olive oil, drained (oil reserved) and broken into chunks	4 ripe tomatoes (about 2 lb/1 kg), peeled, seeded and coarsely chopped (see Tips, below)
1 onion, diced	½ tsp (2 mL) salt (approx.)
½ cup (125 mL) chopped parsley leaves	¼ tsp (1 mL) freshly ground black pepper
½ tsp (2 mL) hot pepper flakes	2 jars (each 6 oz/375 g) marinated artichoke hearts
	12 oz (375 g) cheese tortellini

1 In a wide saucepan, heat 2 tbsp (30 mL) oil from the tuna over medium heat until shimmery. Add onion and cook, stirring often, for about 3 minutes, until softened. Stir in parsley and hot pepper flakes. Stir in tomatoes, salt and pepper. Bring to a simmer, reduce heat to medium-low and simmer, stirring occasionally, for 10 minutes.

2 Drain artichokes and set marinade aside. Coarsely chop artichokes and add to pan along with marinade. Bring to a simmer and cook for 20 minutes, until sauce is thickened.

3 Meanwhile, in a large pot of boiling salted water, cook tortellini over high heat for about 7 minutes, until tender. Drain.

4 Add tortellini and tuna to artichoke mixture. Add salt to taste, if necessary. Let pasta rest for 5 minutes before serving.

TIPS

If you have access to a microwave, brown-bagging leftover pasta is a tasty alternative to packing sandwiches. This sturdy pasta is a good candidate for lunch.

Using a serrated vegetable peeler is a fuss-free way to peel tomatoes.

Substitute an equal quantity of salmon or mackerel for the tuna.

TUNA FETTUCCINE ALFREDO

MAKES 4 SERVINGS • My simple Alfredo sauce adapts to all kinds of pasta and seafood. It's easy to make and kids like it. But it's very creamy, so be careful not to overindulge.

- 12 oz (375 g) whole wheat fettuccine
- ¼ cup (60 mL) unsalted butter
- 2 cloves garlic, minced
- 1 cup (250 mL) heavy or whipping (35%) cream
- 2 cups (500 mL) freshly grated Parmesan cheese (4 oz/125 g; see Tips, below)
- 1 can (6 oz/170 g) tuna in water, drained and broken into chunks
- ¼ cup (60 mL) chopped parsley leaves, divided

1 In a large pot of boiling salted water, cook fettuccine over medium heat for about 12 minutes, until tender to the bite (al dente). Drain.

2 Meanwhile, in a saucepan over medium-low heat, melt butter. Stir in garlic for 20 seconds, then stir in cream. When mixture returns to a simmer, cook for 5 minutes, stirring occasionally. Stir in Parmesan until melted. Stir in tuna and 3 tbsp (45 mL) parsley. Remove from heat.

3 Place fettuccine in warmed individual serving bowls. Ladle sauce over top and sprinkle with remaining parsley.

TIPS

You can use lower-priced flaked tuna — the rich sauce compensates.

I use a kitchen rasp to grate the Parmesan into fluffy flakes. Volume amounts for Parmesan can vary wildly, depending upon how it is packed into the measuring cup and how long it sits, dries out and settles. When possible, go by weight.

Substitute an equal quantity of salmon, mackerel or clams for the tuna.

THE ZITI CAPER

MAKES 4 SERVINGS • Pasta meets tuna, anchovies, beans and caperberries. It's a delectable combination of lively, bold flavors.

12 oz (375 g) ziti

1 tbsp (15 mL) extra virgin olive oil

2 cloves garlic, chopped

2 cups (500 mL) grape tomatoes, halved

1 tin (2 oz/50 g) anchovies, drained (oil reserved) and chopped

2 cans (each 3 oz/85 g) tuna in olive oil

1 can (14 to 19 oz/398 to 540 mL) cranberry beans, rinsed and drained (see Tips, below)

3 tbsp (45 mL) capers, drained

Salt and freshly ground black pepper

12 caperberries with stems (see Tips, below)

1 In a large pot of boiling salted water, cook ziti over high heat for about 15 minutes, until tender to the bite (al dente). Scoop out ½ cup (125 mL) cooking water and set aside. Drain ziti.

2 Meanwhile, in a large skillet, heat extra virgin olive oil over medium-high heat until shimmery. Stir in garlic for 20 seconds. Add tomatoes and anchovies, with their oil, and cook, stirring, for 1 to 2 minutes, until tomatoes soften. Remove from heat.

3 Stir in tuna, with oil, and beans. Add ziti and capers. Season to taste with salt and pepper. Toss. If pasta seems difficult to toss evenly, add enough reserved cooking water to loosen it.

4 Transfer to warmed individual serving bowls. Garnish with caperberries, dividing equally. Serve immediately.

TIPS

When preparing pasta, save some of the cooking water. Use it to moisten or loosen the pasta dish if necessary.

Cranberry beans are also known as romano or borlotti beans. I prefer the 19 ounce (540 mL) can.

Capers are the buds and caperberries the olive-shaped fruit of the caper plant. Caperberries are now sold in many supermarkets, as well as in specialty shops. Leave the stems intact when serving them so diners can pick them up.

Substitute an equal quantity of salmon or mackerel for the tuna and add about 2 tbsp (30 mL) extra virgin olive oil.

PASTA WITH SPICY SALMON AND RAPINI

MAKES 6 SERVINGS • Rapini is also known as broccoli rabe. Its slight bitterness is a fabulous asset in spicy and hearty pastas.

1 lb (500 g) mezzi rigatoni (see Tips, below)
1 bunch rapini (about 1¼ lb/625 g)
⅓ cup (75 mL) extra virgin olive oil
4 cloves garlic, minced
1 tsp (5 mL) hot pepper flakes
1 can (7½ oz/213 g) sockeye salmon, drained, deboned and broken into chunks
1¼ tsp (6 mL) salt (approx.), divided
¼ tsp (1 mL) freshly ground black pepper
½ cup (125 mL) freshly grated Parmesan cheese (1 oz/30 g)

1 In a large pot of boiling salted water, cook rigatoni over medium heat for 12 to 15 minutes, until tender to the bite (al dente). Drain and set aside.

2 Meanwhile, bring a saucepan of salted water to a boil over high heat. Trim off dry bases of rapini stalks and discard. Cut stalks into 1-inch (2.5 cm) lengths. Coarsely chop leaves and florets. Add rapini to boiling water and reduce heat to medium. Cook for about 5 minutes, until stalks are tender-crisp. Drain and rinse under cold running water to stop the cooking. Set aside.

3 In a skillet, heat oil over medium heat. Stir in garlic and hot pepper flakes for 20 seconds. Remove from heat. Stir in salmon, ¼ tsp (1 mL) salt and pepper.

4 In a large warmed serving bowl, toss together rigatoni, rapini and remaining 1 tsp (5 mL) salt. Add salmon mixture and toss gently. Add salt to taste, if necessary. Sprinkle Parmesan evenly over top and serve immediately.

TIPS

Mezzi rigatoni are short, wide tubes. You can use any large, short pasta.

Blanching or cooking rapini in boiling water takes the edge off its bitterness.

VARIATIONS

Add a couple of chopped anchovy fillets with the garlic, and reduce the salt.

If you are not a fan of rapini, use broccoli or broccolini (also known as asparation or baby broccoli).

Substitute an equal quantity of tuna, mackerel or clams for the salmon.

PASTA, RICE & GRAINS

JUMBO SHELLS STUFFED WITH SALMON, RICOTTA AND ZUCCHINI

MAKES 4 SERVINGS • Here's a tasty way to get kids to eat some zucchini while also pleasing the grownups at the dinner table. Everyone loves stuffed pasta shells. The salmon and zucchini add oomph to this popular dish.

Rimmed baking sheet
13- by 9-inch (33 by 23 cm) baking dish

1 package (8 oz/250 g) giant pasta shells

1 tbsp (15 mL) extra virgin olive oil

3 cloves garlic, minced

1 large zucchini (about 8 oz/250 g), trimmed and shredded (see Tips, page 165)

½ tsp (2 mL) salt (approx.)

1 large egg (see Tips, page 165)

2 cups (500 mL) ricotta cheese (1 lb/475 g tub)

1 can (7½ oz/213 g) sockeye salmon, drained, deboned and broken into chunks

1 cup (250 mL) freshly grated Parmesan cheese (2 oz/60 g; see Tips, page 165), divided

1 tbsp (15 mL) chopped fresh dill fronds

⅛ tsp (0.5 mL) freshly ground black pepper

2½ cups (625 mL) prepared marinara sauce (22-ounce/650 mL jar; see Tips, page 165), divided

Preheat oven to 350°F (180°C)

1 In a large pot of boiling salted water over medium heat, cook shells for about 15 minutes, until they are tender but still hold their shape. Drain. Rinse under cold running water to stop the cooking and transfer, open side down in a single layer, to baking sheet to drain.

2 Meanwhile, in a skillet, heat oil over medium heat until shimmery. Stir in garlic. Immediately stir in zucchini and sprinkle with salt. Cook, stirring occasionally and scraping up brown bits from bottom of skillet, for about 8 minutes, until zucchini is tender and turning golden and excess moisture has evaporated. Remove from heat and set aside to cool.

3 In a bowl, using a fork, mix egg, ricotta, salmon, half the Parmesan, dill and pepper. Add salt to taste.

4 Pour all but 1 cup (250 mL) marinara sauce into baking dish. Working with one shell at a time, stuff with 1½ to 2 tbsp (22 to 30 mL) ricotta mixture and place, open side up, in baking dish (you will have about 5 left over). Pour remaining marinara over top. Sprinkle remaining Parmesan evenly over top. Cover with greased foil.

5 Bake in preheated oven for 30 minutes, until sauce is bubbly. Uncover and bake for about 10 minutes more, until cheese is golden. Let casserole rest for 5 to 10 minutes before serving.

TIPS

Bottled marinara sauce speeds up production, but use your own if you have some at hand.

Zucchini is a very wet vegetable. Thanks to shredding and sautéing, however, you can say goodbye to bland, soggy zucchini. Shred it using a box grater.

Large eggs are standard in most test kitchens. However, in some recipes, like this one, the size of the egg is not crucial, so you can use whatever kind you have.

If you have a kitchen scale, go by weight when adding grated Parmesan to a dish. Volume measures vary widely, depending on how the Parmesan is grated, how dry it is and how it is packed into the measuring cup.

 Substitute an equal quantity of tuna, mackerel or kippers for the salmon.

PASTA, RICE & GRAINS

ORZO WITH SALMON, ASPARAGUS AND SMOKED MOZZARELLA

MAKES 4 SERVINGS • Here's a tasty one-pan family dinner that you can whip up quickly. For a flavor boost, rice-shaped orzo can be cooked in stock, like rice. The molten cheese is an added attraction.

- 2 tbsp (30 mL) extra virgin olive oil
- 2 shallots, chopped
- 3 cloves garlic, chopped
- 12 oz (375 g) orzo
- 1½ cups (375 mL) chicken stock
- 1½ cups (375 mL) water
- ¼ tsp (1 mL) salt (approx.)
- 1 bunch asparagus (about 1 lb/500 g), trimmed and cut diagonally into 1-inch (2.5 cm) lengths
- 1½ tsp (7 mL) fresh thyme leaves, divided
- 2 tbsp (30 mL) freshly squeezed lemon juice
- Freshly ground black pepper
- 4 oz (125 g) smoked mozzarella, cut in small dice
- 1 can (7½ oz/213 g) salmon, drained, deboned and broken into chunks

1 In a large saucepan, heat oil over medium heat until shimmery. Add shallots and garlic and cook, stirring often, for 1 to 2 minutes, until softened. Add orzo and cook, stirring often, for 2 minutes. Add stock, water and salt. Bring to a simmer, then reduce heat to medium-low. Cover and cook for 5 minutes. Add asparagus and 1 tsp (5 mL) thyme. Cover and cook for 5 minutes. Stir and cook, uncovered, for 2 minutes more or until liquid is absorbed, orzo is tender to the bite (al dente) and asparagus is tender-crisp.

2 Stir in lemon juice and pepper to taste. Stir in mozzarella until melted. Add salt to taste, if necessary.

3 Transfer to warmed serving plates. Scatter salmon evenly over top, dividing equally. Sprinkle with remaining thyme, dividing equally.

VARIATION

Substitute Israeli couscous, a pearl-shaped pasta, for the orzo. You may have to increase the cooking time.

Substitute an equal quantity of tuna or mackerel for the salmon.

CAESAR SPAGHETTINI

> **MAKES 4 SERVINGS** • Even professed anchovy haters have a soft spot for Caesar salad. I thought Caesar salad flavors would taste good with pasta, and I was right. This dish is a conversation piece. Score another point for anchovies!

12 oz (375 g) spaghettini

¼ cup (60 mL) extra virgin olive oil

4 cloves garlic, minced

1 tin (2 oz/50 g) anchovies (about 15), drained and mashed with a fork

2 tbsp (30 mL) freshly squeezed lemon juice

2 tbsp (30 mL) heavy or whipping (35%) cream

4 cups (1 L) finely shredded romaine hearts (about 8 oz/250 g or 1 small head; see Tips, below)

Salt

2 tsp (10 mL) coarsely ground black pepper

2 oz (60 g) Parmesan cheese, shaved (see Tips, below)

1 In a large pot of boiling salted water, cook spaghettini over medium heat for about 10 minutes, until tender to the bite (al dente). Scoop out about ½ cup (125 mL) cooking water and set aside. Drain pasta.

2 Meanwhile, in a 12-inch (30 cm) skillet, heat oil over medium heat until shimmery. Remove from heat, add garlic and anchovies and stir constantly for 1 minute to prevent burning. Stir in lemon juice and cream.

3 Return skillet to medium-low heat and add spaghettini and romaine. Toss with tongs. If pasta seems dry or difficult to toss evenly with romaine, add enough reserved cooking water to moisten and loosen it. Season to taste with salt.

4 Transfer to a serving platter or warmed individual bowls. Top with pepper, then Parmesan. Serve immediately.

TIPS

When preparing pasta, it is always wise to save some of the cooking water as insurance. This starchy water has thickening and/or emulsifying power if you need it, and it can be used to thin a sauce without making it watery or to help toppings stick to the pasta. If your pasta looks dry or clumpy or is difficult to toss with the toppings or sauce, add some of the cooking water in increments until it is suitably moist. Generally you won't need it for creamy dishes or pastas with abundant sauce.

Romaine hearts are the tender inner leaves. They are sold separately in supermarkets.

Fine Parmesan is a cornerstone of this pasta. Keep the dish uptown and use Parmigiano-Reggiano (known as the "king of cheeses"). Use a cheese slicer or a vegetable peeler to shave the Parmesan thinly off the wedge.

PENNE WITH ANCHOVIED BROCCOLINI

MAKES 4 SERVINGS • For the most lip-smackingly savory pasta, be fearless with your anchovies. They are fabulous with cruciferous veggies such as broccolini.

12 oz (375 g) penne

2 tbsp (30 mL) extra virgin olive oil

2 tins (each 2 oz/50 g) anchovies in extra virgin olive oil, with oil

2 large cloves garlic, minced

1 tbsp (15 mL) finely grated lemon zest

$\frac{1}{4}$ tsp (1 mL) hot pepper flakes

2 bunches broccolini (about 12 oz/375 g total), trimmed, stems cut in 1-inch (2.5 cm) lengths and florets left intact (see Tip, below)

$\frac{1}{8}$ tsp (0.5 mL) freshly ground black pepper

1 cup (250 mL) freshly grated Parmesan cheese (2 oz/60 g)

1 In a large pot of boiling salted water, cook penne over medium heat for about 12 minutes or until tender to the bite (al dente). Scoop out about $\frac{1}{2}$ cup (125 mL) cooking water and set aside. Drain pasta.

2 Meanwhile, in a large skillet, heat oil over medium heat until shimmery. Add anchovies, with their oil, and cook, stirring, for 1 minute, until they start to dissolve. Stir in garlic, lemon zest and hot pepper flakes for 30 seconds. Add broccolini, cover and cook, stirring occasionally, for about 10 minutes, until softened. Uncover and cook, stirring often, for about 2 minutes, until tender-crisp. Sprinkle pepper over top and remove from heat.

3 Add penne and Parmesan and toss well. If pasta seems dry or difficult to toss evenly, add enough reserved cooking water to moisten and loosen it. Serve immediately.

TIP

Broccolini is a cross between broccoli and gai lan, also known as Chinese kale. It is sometimes called baby broccoli because it's more tender than broccoli and not bitter, or asparation, because it tastes and looks like a cross between broccoli and asparagus. The British refer to it as tenderstem broccoli. The spears are topped with small florets and sometimes yellow flowers. It's all edible — you just have to cut about $\frac{1}{4}$ inch (0.5 cm) off the base of each spear.

VARIATION

If you are watching your wallet, substitute an equal quantity of broccoli florets (by weight) instead of using broccolini.

SPANISH NOODLES

MAKES 4 SERVINGS • This love-child of paella and risotto won't win any awards for good looks, but it sure tastes good. I've put it on my comfort-food list.

3 tbsp (45 mL) extra virgin olive oil, divided

12 oz (375 g) vermicelli pasta, broken into 2- to 3-inch (5 to 7.5 cm) segments (see Tips, below)

2 shallots, finely chopped

2 cloves garlic, minced

1 can (14 oz/398 mL) diced tomatoes, drained

4 cups (1 L) chicken stock

2 cups (500 mL) water

1 tsp (5 mL) smoked hot paprika

¼ tsp (1 mL) saffron, crumbled

1 can (5 oz/142 g) surf clams, coarsely chopped

Salt

1 cup (250 mL) sliced pitted green olives (about 15 large)

1 small roasted red pepper, cut in thin strips

1 In a 12-inch (30 cm) skillet, heat 2 tbsp (30 mL) oil over medium heat until shimmery. Add vermicelli and cook, tossing often with tongs, for about 5 minutes, until coated in oil and lightly toasted. Transfer to a bowl.

2 Add remaining 1 tbsp (15 mL) oil to skillet and heat over medium heat until shimmery. Add shallots and cook, stirring often, for about 3 minutes, until softened. Stir in garlic for 20 seconds. Stir in tomatoes. Add stock, water, paprika, saffron and toasted vermicelli. After mixture comes to a boil, cook for about 10 minutes, stirring often, until noodles are just tender and sauce is only slightly soupy.

3 Add clams and reduce heat to low. Cover and cook for about 5 minutes, until noodles have absorbed remaining liquid (the noodles will be moist and sticky, similar to risotto). Stir, scraping up brown bits from bottom of pan. Season to taste with salt.

4 Transfer noodles to a serving dish or individual bowls. Top with olives and roasted pepper strips. Serve immediately.

TIPS

If you can find them, use the short, thin Spanish noodles called fideos, which are sold in specialty shops in some regions.

Freeze the liquid from the tomatoes and stir it into your next soup.

If you prefer, substitute baby clams for the meaty ones. Stir them in at the end.

SPAGHETTI WITH CLAM SAUCE TWO WAYS

MAKES 4 SERVINGS • Fresh clams are good, but if you crave this Neapolitan favorite without the usual fuss and expense, you can make a very respectable version using canned clams. So now your choice is between white clam sauce (*vongole bianco*) or tomatoey clam sauce (*vongole rosso*). As with the New England versus Manhattan clam chowder rivalry (see pages 52 and 53), white has the edge. Which team are you on?

White Sauce

- 12 oz (375 g) spaghetti
- ¼ cup (60 mL) extra virgin olive oil
- 4 large cloves garlic, minced
- ¼ tsp (1 mL) hot pepper flakes
- ½ cup (125 mL) dry white wine
- ½ cup (125 mL) clam juice (see Tips, below)
- 2 tbsp (30 mL) heavy or whipping (35%) cream
- 1 can (5 oz/142 g) chopped surf clams or baby clams, rinsed and drained (see Tips, below)
- ¼ cup + 1 tbsp (75 mL) chopped parsley leaves, divided
- Salt and freshly ground black pepper
- Freshly grated Parmesan cheese, optional

1 In a large pot of boiling salted water over medium heat, cook spaghetti for 10 to 12 minutes, until tender to the bite (al dente). Drain and set aside.

2 Meanwhile, in a large skillet, heat oil over medium heat until shimmery. Remove from heat, add garlic and hot pepper flakes and stir for 1 minute. Stir in wine, clam juice and cream. Return skillet to element and simmer mixture for 5 minutes or until reduced to about ¾ cup (175 mL). Stir in clams and ¼ cup (60 mL) parsley. Season to taste with salt and pepper. Remove from element.

3 Immediately add spaghetti to clam mixture and toss with tongs. Set aside for 5 minutes to absorb liquid.

4 Before serving, adjust the salt to taste, then sprinkle remaining 1 tbsp (15 mL) parsley over top. Serve Parmesan alongside, if using.

TIPS

You can use baby clams or meaty clams. If using the latter (my preference), chop them yourself or buy them already chopped.

For a pasta with bolder flavor, double the amount of clams.

Clam juice, sold in supermarkets, stands in for the liquor that the live clams release during cooking.

Use top-quality extra virgin olive oil and fragrant dry white Italian wine, as they are essential flavorings in this simple dish.

VARIATIONS

Add oomph to this dish by including pancetta in Step 2. Sauté 2 oz (60 g) chopped pancetta in the hot oil until it is golden. Then remove the skillet from the heat and add the garlic and hot pepper flakes. Continue with the recipe.

Instead of using cream, stir in 2 tbsp (30 mL) cold butter after the sauce is reduced, before adding the clams.

Red Sauce

12 oz (375 g) spaghetti

¼ cup (60 mL) extra virgin olive oil

2 oz (60 g) pancetta, chopped (see Tips, below)

4 large cloves garlic

¼ tsp (1 mL) hot pepper flakes

½ cup (125 mL) dry white wine

½ cup (125 mL) clam juice

1 can (14 to 19 oz/398 to 540 mL) diced tomatoes, with juice (see Tips, below)

1 can (5 oz/142 g) chopped surf clams or baby clams, rinsed and drained

¼ cup + 1 tbsp (75 mL) chopped parsley leaves, divided

Salt and freshly ground black pepper

Freshly grated Parmesan cheese, optional

1 In a large pot of boiling salted water over medium heat, cook spaghetti for 10 to 12 minutes, until tender to the bite (al dente). Drain and set aside.

2 Meanwhile, in a large skillet, heat oil over medium heat until shimmery. Add pancetta and cook, stirring, for about 2 minutes, until golden and starting to crisp. Using a slotted spoon, transfer to a small bowl.

3 Remove skillet from heat, add garlic and hot pepper flakes and stir for 1 minute. Stir in wine, clam juice and tomatoes, with juice. Return skillet to element and simmer mixture for 10 minutes or until it is reduced to about 2¼ cups (300 mL). Stir in clams, ¼ cup (60 mL) parsley and salt and pepper to taste. Remove skillet from heat, add spaghetti and toss with tongs. Set aside for 5 minutes to absorb liquid.

4 Before serving, adjust the salt to taste, then sprinkle the pancetta and remaining 1 tbsp (15 mL) parsley over top. Serve Parmesan alongside, if desired.

TIPS

Buy canned diced tomatoes because they hold their shape better in pasta. I prefer the larger, 19-ounce (540 mL) can. If you use the smaller size, save some of the pasta cooking water and add a bit to the spaghetti if necessary.

If you don't have pancetta, omit it or use bacon. Pancetta is not traditional, but its smokiness complements the clams.

Parmesan is not traditionally served with fish or seafood pasta, but who cares? Add as much as you like.

CLAM CARBONARA

MAKES 4 TO 6 SERVINGS • Carbonara is basically spaghetti with bacon and eggs. No wonder it tastes so good! The addition of clams puts this luscious dish right over the top.

- 1 lb (500 g) spaghetti
- 8 oz (250 g) pancetta, cut in ¼-inch (0.5 cm) dice
- 2 cloves garlic, minced
- ½ cup (125 mL) diced green bell pepper (⅛ inch/3 mm)
- 8 oz (250 g) cremini mushrooms, sliced (3 cups/750 mL)
- ¼ cup (60 mL) dry white wine
- 1 can (5 oz/142 g) baby clams, rinsed and drained (see Tip, below)
- 4 large eggs
- ½ cup (125 mL) half-and-half (10%) cream
- 1 cup (250 mL) freshly grated Parmesan cheese (2 oz/60 g)
- Salt and freshly ground black pepper
- 1 tbsp (15 mL) finely chopped parsley leaves

1 In a large pot of boiling salted water, cook spaghetti over medium heat until tender to the bite (al dente), 12 to 15 minutes. Drain pasta.

2 Meanwhile, in a 12-inch (30 cm) skillet over medium heat, cook pancetta, stirring, until it starts to brown, about 5 minutes. Stir in garlic. Add bell pepper and mushrooms. Cook, stirring, until mushrooms release their liquid and start to brown, about 5 minutes. Stir in wine, scraping up brown bits from bottom of skillet. Add pasta and toss briefly until coated and hot. Add clams. Remove from heat.

3 In a bowl, whisk eggs. In a small pan over medium heat (or in a measuring cup on High in the microwave), heat cream for about 1 minute, until scalded (do not allow it to boil). Whisking constantly, gradually add cream to eggs. Whisk in Parmesan.

4 Add egg mixture to hot spaghetti and toss to coat evenly and thoroughly. Season to taste with salt and pepper.

5 Transfer to warm serving bowls. Sprinkle parsley over top and serve immediately.

TIP
You can use larger, meatier clams instead of the baby ones.

Substitute tuna, salmon or mackerel for the clams.

PASTA, RICE & GRAINS

FISHBALLS BRAISED IN WHITE WINE TOMATO BASIL SAUCE

MAKES 4 TO 6 SERVINGS • Forget spaghetti and meatballs — try spaghetti and fishballs. This saucy dish is your ticket to a variety of meals. Serve it over pasta or rice, or slice up some crusty bread to serve alongside.

Rimmed baking sheet, lined with generously greased foil
8-inch (20 cm) square baking dish

FISHBALLS

2 cans (each 7½ oz/213 g) salmon, drained, deboned and broken into chunks
2 large eggs
¼ cup (60 mL) panko bread crumbs
1 clove garlic, minced
1 tbsp (15 mL) unsalted butter, melted and cooled, optional (see Tips, page 175)
2 tsp (10 mL) finely chopped parsley leaves
1 tsp (5 mL) finely grated lemon zest
½ tsp (2 mL) hot pepper flakes
⅛ tsp (0.5 mL) salt
⅛ tsp (0.5 mL) freshly ground black pepper

SAUCE

2 tbsp (30 mL) extra virgin olive oil
1 onion, diced
1 clove garlic, finely chopped
1 carrot (about 2 oz/60 g), chopped
½ cup (125 mL) dry white wine
1 can (28 oz/796 mL) plum tomatoes, with juice, puréed (see Tips, page 175)
¾ cup (175 mL) chicken stock
1 tbsp (15 mL) granulated sugar
2 tbsp (30 mL) chopped basil leaves
1 tbsp (15 mL) chopped fresh oregano leaves
1 bay leaf
¼ tsp (1 mL) salt (approx.)
⅛ tsp (0.5 mL) freshly ground black pepper
Freshly grated Parmesan cheese

Preheat oven to 350°F (180°C)

1 **FISHBALLS:** Gently squeeze excess moisture from salmon and place it in a bowl. Add eggs, panko crumbs, garlic, butter, if using, parsley, lemon zest, hot pepper flakes, salt and pepper. Mash with a fork until blended.

2 With greased hands, shape salmon mixture into 1-inch (2.5 cm) balls and place on prepared baking sheet as completed. (You should have about 35.)

3 Bake in preheated oven for 10 minutes. Turn and bake for 10 minutes more. Remove from oven and set aside for 5 minutes to firm up. Lower oven temperature to 325°F (160°C).

4 SAUCE: Meanwhile, in a skillet, heat oil over medium heat until shimmery. Add onion, garlic and carrot and cook, stirring often, for 5 minutes, until vegetables soften. Stir in wine, scraping brown bits from bottom of pan. Stir in tomatoes, stock, sugar, basil, oregano, bay leaf, salt and pepper. Bring to a boil. Reduce heat and simmer for 10 minutes, until slightly thickened.

5 Transfer fishballs to baking dish. Ladle sauce over top, shaking dish gently to distribute evenly. Bake in preheated oven for 1 hour, until sauce is thick. Discard bay leaf and gently stir together fishballs and sauce. Taste and adjust the salt.

6 Sprinkle Parmesan, to taste, evenly over top and serve immediately.

TIPS

To purée the tomatoes, pulse them, with their juices, for a few seconds in a food processor.

This recipe will work with pink salmon but I prefer using sockeye salmon because it is moister and more flavorful.

Fishballs have a tendency to become dry. The butter moistens them, but this recipe will work fine without it.

VARIATION

Add 2 tbsp (30 mL) dry grated Parmesan cheese to the fishball mixture in Step 1.

LEMONY SALMON AND ASPARAGUS RISOTTO

MAKES 4 TO 6 SERVINGS • Risotto comes in many glorious guises. This variation pairs salmon, asparagus and fresh herbs for a springtime meal.

- 5 cups (1.25 L) chicken or vegetable stock
- 1 cup (250 mL) water
- 8 oz (250 g) asparagus, trimmed and cut into 1-inch (2.5 cm) segments
- 1 tbsp (15 mL) unsalted butter
- 1 tbsp (15 mL) extra virgin olive oil
- 1 onion, diced
- 1½ cups (375 mL) Arborio rice (see Tips, page 177)
- 2 tsp (10 mL) finely grated lemon zest
- 2 tbsp (30 mL) freshly squeezed lemon juice
- Freshly ground white pepper
- 2 tbsp (30 mL) coarsely chopped parsley, divided
- 1 tbsp (15 mL) chopped fresh dill fronds
- 2 tbsp (30 mL) heavy or whipping (35%) cream
- ½ cup (125 mL) freshly grated Parmesan cheese (1 oz/30 g)
- Salt
- 1 can (7½ oz/213 g) salmon, drained, deboned and broken into chunks

1 In a saucepan over medium-high heat, bring stock and water to a boil. Add asparagus. Reduce heat to medium-low and simmer for 5 to 7 minutes, until tender-crisp. Using a mesh scoop, transfer asparagus to a small bowl. Remove pan from heat and place on a back burner.

2 In another saucepan, melt butter with oil over medium heat. Add onion and cook, stirring often, for about 5 minutes, until it starts to turn golden. Add rice and stir for 1 minute, until coated.

3 Reduce heat to medium-low. Add stock mixture 1 cup (250 mL) at a time, stirring often. Do not add liquid until previous addition is almost absorbed. Repeat until all the liquid has been used and rice is creamy and tender but firm. This should take 20 to 30 minutes (see Tips, page 177).

4 Remove pan from heat. Stir in asparagus, lemon zest and juice, pepper to taste, 1 tbsp (15 mL) parsley and dill. Stir in cream and Parmesan. Add salt to taste. Scatter salmon over top. Cover pan and let risotto rest for 5 minutes, then mix gently. Sprinkle remaining 1 tbsp (15 mL) parsley over top. Serve immediately.

TIPS

Risotto is traditionally made with hot stock. However, you don't have to keep the stock simmering. Even room-temperature stock will work.

I find store-bought stock (particularly vegetable stock) too aggressive, so I water it down.

The speed at which risotto cooks depends on the width of the pan, the heat level and the temperature of the stock.

Risotto is traditionally finished with butter, but heavy cream is a smooth, satiny alternative.

Substitute an equal quantity of tuna or clams for the salmon.

TUNA AND SPINACH RISOTTO

> **MAKES 4 TO 6 SERVINGS** • Risotto is a popular dish for both everyday suppers and dinner parties. You can make good risotto with canned seafood. Here is one simple idea.

5 cups (1.25 L) chicken or vegetable stock

1 cup (250 mL) water

2 cans (each 3 oz/85 g) tuna in olive oil, drained (oil reserved) and broken into chunks (see Tips, below)

1½ cups (375 mL) Arborio rice (see Tips, below)

2 cloves garlic, minced

¼ cup (60 mL) dry white wine

1 tbsp (15 mL) unsalted butter

2½ cups (625 mL) thinly sliced spinach leaves (2 oz/60 g)

1 tsp (5 mL) finely grated lemon zest

Freshly ground black pepper

½ cup (125 mL) freshly grated Parmesan cheese (1 oz/30 g)

1 In a saucepan over medium-high heat, bring stock and water to a boil. Remove from heat and place on a back burner.

2 Pour 2 tbsp (30 mL) of the oil drained from the tuna into another saucepan and heat over medium heat until shimmery. Add rice and cook, stirring often, for 3 to 5 minutes, until rice is toasted and turning golden. Stir in garlic for 10 seconds. Stir in wine until it evaporates. Reduce heat to medium-low. Add stock mixture 1 cup (250 mL) at a time, stirring often. Do not add liquid until previous addition is almost absorbed. Repeat until all the liquid has been used and rice is creamy and tender but firm. This should take 20 to 30 minutes.

3 Remove from heat. Stir in butter, spinach, lemon zest and pepper. Stir in tuna and Parmesan cheese. Serve immediately.

TIPS

Risotto rice is short-grained, creamy and starchy. Arborio (used here) is most popular, while Carnaroli and Vialone Nano are pricier.

The speed at which risotto cooks depends on the width of the pan, the heat level and the temperature of the stock.

If you've purchased a package containing three small cans of tuna, feel free to add the third can.

Substitute an equal quantity of salmon or mackerel for the tuna.

PASTA, RICE & GRAINS

EASY HAM AND CLAM JAMBALAYA

MAKES 4 TO 6 SERVINGS • This plain one-pot dinner won't win any haute cuisine awards, but it's mighty good on the family dinner table.

- 1 tbsp (15 mL) extra virgin olive oil
- 1 small onion, diced
- 2 cloves garlic, minced
- 1 stalk celery, chopped
- ½ green bell pepper, chopped
- 1 cup (250 mL) basmati rice, rinsed (see Tips, below)
- 8 oz (250 g) chunk smoked ham, cut in ½-inch (1 cm) cubes
- 1 cup (250 mL) okra cut in ½-inch (1 cm) segments (about 4 oz/125 g)
- 1 cup (250 mL) chicken or vegetable stock
- 1 bottle (8 oz/240 mL) clam juice
- 2 tsp (10 mL) Cajun seasoning
- 1 can (5 oz/142 g) surf or meaty clams, coarsely chopped
- 1 can (14 oz/398 mL) diced tomatoes, drained (see Tips, below)
- Salt and freshly ground black pepper
- Cayenne pepper
- 1 tbsp (15 mL) chopped parsley leaves

1 In a saucepan, heat oil over medium heat until shimmery. Add onion, garlic, celery and green pepper and cook, stirring often, for about 3 minutes, until vegetables soften. Add rice and stir for 1 minute, until coated. Add ham, okra, stock, clam juice and Cajun seasoning and stir well. Bring to a simmer, reduce heat to low, cover and simmer for about 18 minutes, until rice is just tender and liquid has been absorbed.

2 Arrange clams and tomatoes evenly over top. Set pan aside, uncovered, for 5 minutes. Season to taste with salt and pepper and mix gently. Before serving, sprinkle with cayenne to taste and parsley.

TIPS

Stick to diced tomatoes in this recipe — they will hold their shape better, so the dish looks neater. Drain them well.

I like to use basmati rice because it doesn't get as sticky or clumpy as generic white rice, but you can substitute.

VARIATIONS

Switch to andouille sausage instead of ham.

You can use baby clams for this recipe.

PORTUGUESE RICE WITH CLAMS

MAKES 4 SERVINGS • My kind Portuguese neighbors taught me the secrets to making this zesty rice. Although it is usually served as a side dish, it's worth adding seafood to make this a meal. Add a green salad as accompaniment.

1 cup (250 mL) long-grain white rice, rinsed

2 cups (500 mL) water

Salt

¼ cup (60 mL) extra virgin olive oil

½ cup (125 mL) minced red bell pepper

1 shallot, minced

¼ cup (60 mL) skinned, finely chopped chouriço or linguiça sausage

1 clove garlic, minced

2 tbsp (30 mL) tomato paste

1 can (5 oz/142 g) surf or meaty clams, rinsed, drained and coarsely chopped

Piri piri sauce, optional (see Tips, below)

Freshly ground black pepper

2 tbsp (30 mL) chopped parsley leaves

16 to 20 black olives (see Tips, below)

1 In a saucepan over high heat, bring rice, water and salt, to taste, to a boil. Reduce heat to low. Cover and simmer for about 18 minutes, until rice is tender and water has been absorbed. Remove from heat. Fluff rice with a fork and let rest, uncovered, for 5 minutes.

2 Meanwhile, in a small saucepan, heat oil over medium-low heat until shimmery. Add red pepper and shallot and cook, stirring often, for about 10 minutes, until vegetables are very soft. (Do not brown the vegetables. Lower the heat if necessary — the mixture should poach rather than fry.) Add sausage and garlic and cook, stirring often, for 5 minutes. Stir in tomato paste.

3 Add clams and vegetable mixture to rice and mix gently with a fork. Add piri piri sauce (if using), salt and pepper to taste. Garnish with parsley and scatter olives over top. Serve immediately.

TIPS

Make sure the vegetables are minced very finely. The red pepper should be almost puréed.

Piri piri is Portuguese hot pepper sauce.

The olives are usually tossed on the rice whole, but you can pit them if you wish.

VARIATIONS

Portuguese sausages come in mild and spicy versions. I start with the mild kind and add heat with piri piri sauce. However, you can start with spicy sausage instead.

The rice should be firm, not sticky. You can use converted (parboiled) rice if you prefer.

MOROCCAN-STYLE SALMON QUINOA

MAKES 4 SERVINGS • Make an exotic quinoa pilaf with just a can of fish and supermarket ingredients. This is healthy as well as delicious.

1 cup (250 mL) quinoa, rinsed and drained	⅛ tsp (0.5 mL) ground cinnamon
1 cup (250 mL) chicken or vegetable stock	1 can (7½ oz/213 g) salmon, drained, deboned and broken into chunks
1 cup (250 mL) water	½ cup (125 mL) dried apricots (12), coarsely chopped
2 tbsp (30 mL) extra virgin olive oil	½ cup (125 mL) diced red onion
1 tbsp (15 mL) freshly squeezed lemon juice	¼ cup (60 mL) chopped parsley leaves
1 clove garlic, minced	¼ cup (60 mL) chopped cilantro leaves
½ tsp (2 mL) salt (approx.)	2 tbsp (30 mL) chopped mint leaves
¼ tsp (1 mL) ground cumin	¼ cup (60 mL) pine nuts, toasted (see Tip, below)
⅛ tsp (0.5 mL) freshly ground black pepper	

1 In a dry skillet over medium heat, toast quinoa, stirring, for 5 minutes, until it smells nutty and no longer steams. Carefully add stock (the mixture will sputter) and water. Once mixture comes to a full boil, reduce heat to medium-low, cover and simmer for 15 minutes, until quinoa is tender-firm and liquid has been absorbed. Remove from heat, fluff with a fork and set aside, uncovered, for 5 minutes. Transfer to a large serving bowl.

2 Meanwhile, in a small bowl, whisk together oil, lemon juice, garlic, salt, cumin, pepper and cinnamon. Pour over quinoa and mix with a fork. Add salmon, apricots, onion, parsley, cilantro and mint. Mix gently. Add salt to taste, if necessary. Sprinkle with pine nuts.

3 Serve warm or at room temperature, or cover and refrigerate overnight.

TIP

Toast pine nuts in a dry skillet on medium heat for 2 to 3 minutes, until fragrant and golden.

Substitute an equal quantity of tuna or crab for the salmon.

CITRUS QUINOA WITH CRAB AND CRESS

MAKES 2 TO 4 SERVINGS • Seafood and citrus have had a long and happy relationship. This uptown quinoa dish smells fragrant and tastes sublime. It is quick to prepare if you multitask by prepping the remaining ingredients while the quinoa cooks.

- 1 cup (250 mL) quinoa, rinsed and drained
- 1¼ cups (300 mL) chicken or vegetable stock
- ¾ cup (175 mL) freshly squeezed orange juice (2 oranges)
- 1 tsp (5 mL) finely grated lemon zest
- 1 tsp (5 mL) finely grated lime zest
- 2 tbsp (30 mL) extra virgin olive oil
- 1 to 2 tbsp (15 to 30 mL) freshly squeezed lime juice, divided
- 1 tsp (5 mL) liquid honey
- ½ tsp (2 mL) salt (approx.)
- ⅛ tsp (0.5 mL) freshly ground black pepper
- ¼ tsp (1 mL) ground cumin
- 1 clove garlic, minced
- 1 can (4¼ oz/120 g) crabmeat, rinsed and drained (see Tip, below)
- 2 cups (500 mL) watercress leaves

1 In a dry skillet over medium heat, toast quinoa, stirring, for 5 minutes, until it smells nutty and no longer steams. Carefully add stock (the mixture will sputter), then orange juice and lemon and lime zest. Once mixture comes to a full boil, reduce heat to medium-low, cover and simmer for 15 minutes, until quinoa is tender-firm and liquid has been absorbed. Remove from heat, fluff with a fork and set aside, uncovered, for 5 minutes. Transfer to a large serving bowl.

2 Meanwhile, in a small bowl, whisk together oil, 1 tbsp (15 mL) lime juice, honey, salt, pepper, cumin and garlic. Pour over quinoa and mix with a fork. Add crab and watercress and mix gently. Add salt to taste, if necessary, and some or all of the remaining 1 tbsp (15 mL) lime juice, to taste.

3 Serve warm or at room temperature.

TIP

Small-chunk shelf-stable crab is fine in this, but avoid ultra-flaky "salad" crab. Alternatively, dress up this dish with premium lump crabmeat.

Substitute an equal quantity of tuna or salmon for the crab.

Library and Archives Canada Cataloguing in Publication

Title: Tinned fish pantry cookbook : 100 recipes from tuna & salmon to crab & more / Susan Sampson.

Other titles: 100 recipes from tuna & salmon to crab & more | One hundred recipes from tuna & salmon to crab & more

Names: Sampson, Susan, author.

Description: Includes index.

Identifiers: Canadiana 20200387111 | ISBN 9780778806813 (softcover)

Subjects: LCSH: Cooking (Seafood) | LCSH: Cooking (Fish) | LCSH: Cooking (Canned foods) | LCGFT: Cookbooks.

Classification: LCC TX747 .S348 2021 | DDC 641.6/92—dc23

INDEX

A

anchovies, 18–19
  Bagna Cauda Dip, 34
  Caesar Salad Two Ways, 82
  Caesar Spaghettini, 167
  Hungarian Cheese Spread on Rye, 101
  Penne with Anchovied Broccolini, 168
  Salade Niçoise, 78
  Tuna Muffuletta Sandwiches, 90
  Tuna Tapenade, 32
  The Ziti Caper, 162
anchovy paste, 19
  Niçoise Tuna Burgers, 112
appetizers, 31–43
artichoke hearts
  Niçoise Tuna Burgers, 112
  Pan Bagnat, 93
  Salade Niçoise, 78
  Tortellini Toss-Up, 160
  Tuna and Artichoke Panini, 96
arugula
  Sardines with Roast Spuds, Smoked Paprika Oil and Lemon, 42
  Tuna and Bean Salad on Arugula, 72
  Tuscan Tuna Rolls, 94
Asian Stock, 54
asparagus
  Crab Louis (variation), 69
  Lemony Salmon and Asparagus Risotto, 176
  Orzo with Salmon, Asparagus and Smoked Mozzarella, 166

avocado
  Salmon, Avocado and Red Onion Club Sandwiches, 98
  Tuna Cobb Salad, 71

B

bacon and pancetta
  Caesar Salad Two Ways, 82
  CBLT, 100
  Clam, Bacon and Chive Dip, 35
  Clam Carbonara, 173
  Clam Pie, 142
  Louisiana Clams and Corn, 136
  Manhattan Clam Chowder, 53
  New England Clam Chowder, 52
  Salmon, Avocado and Red Onion Club Sandwiches, 98
  Spaghetti with Clam Sauce Two Ways, 170
  Tuna Cobb Salad, 71
Bagna Cauda Dip, 34
beans. *See also* beans, green/yellow
  Pasta with Tuna, Beans, Sage and Olives, 155
  Salmon and White Bean Soup with Oniony Croutons, 46
  Soba Noodles with Fishballs and Snow Peas (variation), 56
  Tuna and Bean Salad on Arugula, 72
  Tuna Taco Salad, 73

Tuscan Tuna Rolls, 94
The Ziti Caper, 162
beans, green/yellow
  Italian Tuna, Potato and Green Bean Salad, 76
  Salade Niçoise, 78
  Today's Tuna Noodle Casserole, 130
  Tuna, Egg and Fresh Bean Salad, 75
bonito, 14
bread (as ingredient). *See also* burgers; sandwiches and wraps
  Crabby Cakes, 121
  Deviled Crab, 138
  Salmon and Roasted Garlic Bisque with Cajun Croutons, 48
  Salmon and White Bean Soup with Oniony Croutons, 46
  Salmon Loaf, 126
  Sicilian-Style Sardine Pasta, 152
  Today's Tuna Noodle Casserole, 130
broccoli and broccolini
  Pasta with Spicy Salmon and Rapini (variation), 163
  Penne with Anchovied Broccolini, 168
  Today's Tuna Noodle Casserole (variation), 130
burgers, 112–20

C

Caesar Salad Two Ways, 82
Caesar Spaghettini, 167

California Salmon Salad, 80
canned fish, 25–29
 bones in, 28
 health issues, 27, 29
 oil-packed, 28
 rinsing, 29
 sources, 27
 storing, 26
carrots. *See also* vegetables
 Clam Pie, 142
 Fishballs Braised in White Wine Tomato Basil Sauce, 174
 Soba Noodles with Fishballs and Snow Peas, 56
 Tuna à la King, 134
Catalan Clams and Ham, 36
CBLT, 100
celery. *See also* vegetables
 Crab Étouffé, 137
 Italian Tuna, Potato and Green Bean Salad, 76
 Retro Tuna Salad Pasta, 84
 Salmon Picadillo, 135
 Today's Tuna Noodle Casserole, 130
 Tuna and Bean Salad on Arugula, 72
 Vintage Tuna Salad, 64
cheese. *See also* cream cheese; *specific cheeses (below)*
 Couscous with Tuna, Feta and Lemon Mint Dressing, 85
 Hungarian Cheese Spread on Rye, 101
 Jumbo Shells Stuffed with Salmon, Ricotta and Zucchini, 164
 Today's Tuna Noodle Casserole, 130
 Tuna Cobb Salad, 71
 Tuna McMelts, 89
 Tuna Muffuletta Sandwiches, 90
cheese, Cheddar
 Diner Tuna Melts, 88
 Hot Crab Dip, 33
 Vintage Tuna Mac and Cheese, 157

cheese, Jack
 Salmon, Corn and Herb Chowder with Pepper Jack, 50
 Tuna Taco Salad, 73
cheese, mozzarella
 Orzo with Salmon, Asparagus and Smoked Mozzarella, 166
 Salmon and Sprout Quesadillas, 107
 Sardines Caprese, 77
 Tuna and Artichoke Panini, 96
cheese, Parmesan
 Caesar Salad Two Ways, 82
 Caesar Spaghettini, 167
 Clam Carbonara, 173
 Fishballs Braised in White Wine Tomato Basil Sauce (variation), 174
 Lemony Salmon and Asparagus Risotto, 176
 Parmesan Tuna Sandwiches, 95
 Pasta with Spicy Salmon and Rapini, 163
 Penne with Anchovied Broccolini, 168
 Tuna and Spinach Risotto, 178
 Tuna Fettuccine Alfredo, 161
 Tuna Tetrazzini, 132
Citrus Quinoa with Crab and Cress, 182
clams and clam juice, 21–22
 Catalan Clams and Ham, 36
 Clam, Bacon and Chive Dip, 35
 Clam Carbonara, 173
 Clam Pie, 142
 Clams in Herb Broth with Angel Hair Pasta, 51
 Easy Ham and Clam Jambalaya, 179
 Louisiana Clams and Corn, 136
 Manhattan Clam Chowder, 53

New England Clam Chowder, 52
Portuguese Rice with Clams, 180
Spaghetti with Clam Sauce Two Ways, 170
Spanish Noodles, 169
coconut milk/cream
 Coconut Tuna and Pea Curry, 149
 Thai Coconut Crab Soup, 59
 Thai Curry Salmon Burgers, 120
corn
 Crab and Corn Griddle Cakes, 43
 Louisiana Clams and Corn, 136
 Salmon, Corn and Herb Chowder with Pepper Jack, 50
 Shortcut Tuna Pot Pie, 146
coulibiac (Russian Salmon Pie), 140
couscous
 Couscous with Tuna, Feta and Lemon Mint Dressing, 85
 Orzo with Salmon, Asparagus and Smoked Mozzarella (variation), 166
crabmeat, 19–21
 CBLT, 100
 Citrus Quinoa with Crab and Cress, 182
 Crab, Watercress and Egg Drop Soup, 58
 Crab and Corn Griddle Cakes, 43
 Crabby Cakes, 121
 Crab Étouffé, 137
 Crab Louis, 69
 Creamy Crab and Poblano Soup, 60
 Curried Scrambled Eggs and Crab, 39
 Deviled Crab, 138
 Jamaican Crab and Okra Curry, 147

Thai Coconut Crab Soup, 59
cream. *See also* milk; sour cream
   Clam Carbonara, 173
   Clam Pie, 142
   Crab Étouffé, 137
   Creamy Crab and Poblano Soup, 60
   New England Clam Chowder, 52
   Salmon, Corn and Herb Chowder with Pepper Jack, 50
   Salmon and Roasted Garlic Bisque with Cajun Croutons, 48
   Tuna à la King, 134
   Tuna Fettuccine Alfredo, 161
cream cheese
   Clam, Bacon and Chive Dip, 35
   Hot Crab Dip, 33
   Salmon and Egg Smørrebrød, 41
   Tuna Tapenade (variation), 32
   Tuna Tetrazzini, 132
Creamy Caesar Dressing, 82
cucumber
   Couscous with Tuna, Feta and Lemon Mint Dressing, 85
   Minty Cucumber Dip, 121, 124
   Pan Bagnat, 93
   Salade Niçoise, 78
   Salmon and Egg Smørrebrød, 41
   Seafood Summer Rolls, 108
   Thai Tuna Salad, 74
   Tuna Taco Salad, 73
Curried Scrambled Eggs and Crab, 39

D

Deviled Crab, 138
Deviled Eggs with Tuna, 37
Diner Tuna Melts, 88
dips and spreads, 32–35, 121, 124

E

Easy Ham and Clam Jambalaya, 179
eggs
   Anchovy Egg Salad, Tomato and Sprouts in Pitas, 102
   Clam Carbonara, 173
   Crab, Watercress and Egg Drop Soup, 58
   Crab Louis, 69
   Curried Scrambled Eggs and Crab, 39
   Deviled Eggs with Tuna, 37
   Niçoise Tuna Burgers, 112
   Pan Bagnat, 93
   Russian Salmon Pie, 140
   Salade Niçoise, 78
   Salmon, Spinach and Sweet Potato Frittata, 38
   Salmon and Egg Smørrebrød, 41
   Salmon Loaf, 126
   Tuna, Egg and Fresh Bean Salad, 75
   Tuna Cobb Salad, 71
   Tuna McMelts, 89

F

Faux Pho, 54
fennel
   Manhattan Clam Chowder, 53
   Sicilian-Style Sardine Pasta, 152
Fishballs Braised in White Wine Tomato Basil Sauce, 174
Fish Tacos, 104
French Dressing, Homemade, 71
fruit. *See also* lemon; lime
   California Salmon Salad, 80
   Citrus Quinoa with Crab and Cress, 182
   Moroccan-Style Salmon Quinoa, 181
   Salmon Picadillo, 135

G

garlic
   Bagna Cauda Dip, 34
   Caesar Salad Two Ways, 82
   Caesar Spaghettini, 167
   Salmon and Roasted Garlic Bisque with Cajun Croutons, 48
   Spaghetti with Clam Sauce Two Ways, 170
   Tuna Muffuletta Sandwiches, 90
   Tuna Pantry Pasta, 158
   Tuna Tapenade, 32
ginger
   Salmon Burgers with Honey Ginger Mayo, 116
   Soba Noodles with Fishballs and Snow Peas, 56
   Thai Coconut Crab Soup, 59
   Thai Tuna Salad, 74
Greek Tuna Salad, 67
greens. *See also* sprouts; *specific greens*
   California Salmon Salad, 80
   Fish Tacos, 104
   Pasta with Spicy Salmon and Rapini, 163
   Salmon Burgers with Honey Ginger Mayo, 116
   Tuna Cobb Salad, 71

H

ham
   Catalan Clams and Ham, 36
   Easy Ham and Clam Jambalaya, 179
   Hot Crab Dip, 33
   Hungarian Cheese Spread on Rye, 101

I

Indian Tuna Salad, 67
Italian Tuna, Potato and Green Bean Salad, 76

J

Jamaican Crab and Okra Curry, 147
Jerk Salmon Sliders, 118
Jumbo Shells Stuffed with Salmon, Ricotta and Zucchini, 164

K

kippers, 23

L

leeks
   Russian Salmon Pie, 140
   Salmon and Leek Pot Pie, 144
   Today's Tuna Noodle Casserole, 130
   Vintage Creamed Salmon on Toast, 99
lemon
   Citrus Quinoa with Crab and Cress, 182
   Lemony Salmon and Asparagus Risotto, 176
   New England Clam Chowder, 52
   Niçoise Tuna Burgers, 112
   Salmon Loaf, 126
   Salmon Salad, Classic, 68
   Sardines with Roast Spuds, Smoked Paprika Oil and Lemon, 42
   Tuna Pantry Pasta, 158
lettuce. *See also* greens
   Caesar Salad Two Ways, 82
   Caesar Spaghettini, 167
   CBLT, 100
   Crab Louis, 69
   Pan Bagnat, 93
   Salade Niçoise, 78
   Tuna, Egg and Fresh Bean Salad, 75
   Tuna Taco Salad, 73
lime
   CBLT, 100
   Citrus Quinoa with Crab and Cress, 182
   Clam, Bacon and Chive Dip, 35
   Hot Crab Dip, 33
   Jerk Salmon Sliders, 118
   Salmon Salad, Classic (variation), 68
   Thai Coconut Crab Soup, 59
   Thai Tuna Salad, 74
lobster, 23
Louisiana Clams and Corn, 136

M

mackerel, 22
Manhattan Clam Chowder, 53
mayonnaise (as ingredient)
   CBLT, 100
   Crab Louis, 69
   Creamy Caesar Dressing, 82
   Deviled Eggs with Tuna, 37
   Fish Tacos, 104
   Jerk Salmon Sliders, 118
   Niçoise Tuna Burgers, 112
   Retro Tuna Salad Pasta, 84
   Salmon Burgers with Honey Ginger Mayo, 116
   Salmon Salad, Classic, 68
   Tuna Salad Three Ways, 66
   Tuna Tapenade (variation), 32
   Vintage Tuna Salad, 64
milk. *See also* cream
   Deviled Crab, 138
   Salmon and Leek Pot Pie, 144
   Today's Tuna Noodle Casserole, 130
   Vintage Creamed Salmon on Toast, 99
   Vintage Tuna Mac and Cheese, 157
Minty Cucumber Dip, 124
Moroccan-Style Salmon Quinoa, 181
mushrooms and mushroom soup
   Clam Carbonara, 173
   Russian Salmon Pie, 140
   Soba Noodles with Fishballs and Snow Peas, 56
   Today's Tuna Noodle Casserole, 130
   Tuna à la King, 134
   Tuna Tetrazzini, 132
   Vintage Tuna Mac and Cheese, 157
mussels, 23

N

New England Clam Chowder, 52
Niçoise Tuna Burgers, 112
noodles. *See also* pasta
   Faux Pho, 54
   Soba Noodles with Fishballs and Snow Peas, 56
   Today's Tuna Noodle Casserole, 130
nuts
   California Salmon Salad, 80
   Moroccan-Style Salmon Quinoa, 181
   Nutty Salmon and Spinach Wraps, 103
   Salmon Picadillo, 135
   Thai Tuna Salad, 74
   Tuna Tetrazzini, 132

O

octopus, 23
okra
   Easy Ham and Clam Jambalaya, 179
   Jamaican Crab and Okra Curry, 147
   Louisiana Clams and Corn, 136

olives
- Greek Tuna Salad, 67
- Italian Tuna, Potato and Green Bean Salad, 76
- Italian Tuna Salad, 66
- Niçoise Tuna Burgers, 112
- Olive Dressing, 93
- Pasta with Tuna, Beans, Sage and Olives, 155
- Portuguese Rice with Clams, 180
- Retro Tuna Salad Pasta (variation), 84
- Salade Niçoise, 78
- Salmon Picadillo, 135
- Spanish Noodles, 169
- Tuna and Olive Rotini, 156
- Tuna Muffuletta Sandwiches, 90
- Tuna Tapenade, 32

onions. *See also* onions, green
- Salade Niçoise, 78
- Salmon, Avocado and Red Onion Club Sandwiches, 98
- Thai Tuna Salad, 74

onions, green
- California Salmon Salad, 80
- Hungarian Cheese Spread on Rye, 101
- Louisiana Clams and Corn, 136
- Salmon Picadillo, 135
- Soba Noodles with Fishballs and Snow Peas, 56
- Tuna and Bean Salad on Arugula, 72

Open Sesame Salmon Burgers, 115
Orzo with Salmon, Asparagus and Smoked Mozzarella, 166
oysters, 23

P

Pan Bagnat, 93
pancetta. *See* bacon and pancetta
Parmesan Tuna Sandwiches, 95
pasta. *See also* noodles
- cooking, 154
- Caesar Spaghettini, 167
- Clam Carbonara, 173
- Clams in Herb Broth with Angel Hair Pasta, 51
- Jumbo Shells Stuffed with Salmon, Ricotta and Zucchini, 164
- Orzo with Salmon, Asparagus and Smoked Mozzarella, 166
- Pasta with Spicy Salmon and Rapini, 163
- Pasta with Tuna, Beans, Sage and Olives, 155
- Penne with Anchovied Broccolini, 168
- Retro Tuna Salad Pasta, 84
- Sicilian-Style Sardine Pasta, 152
- Spaghetti with Clam Sauce Two Ways, 170
- Spanish Noodles, 169
- Tortellini Toss-Up, 160
- Tuna and Olive Rotini, 156
- Tuna Fettuccine Alfredo, 161
- Tuna Tetrazzini, 132
- Vintage Tuna Mac and Cheese, 157
- The Ziti Caper, 162

peas (green)
- Coconut Tuna and Pea Curry, 149
- Faux Pho, 54
- Shortcut Tuna Pot Pie, 146
- Soba Noodles with Fishballs and Snow Peas, 56
- Today's Tuna Noodle Casserole (variation), 130
- Vintage Creamed Salmon on Toast, 99

Penne with Anchovied Broccolini, 168
peppers, bell. *See also* peppers, chile; vegetables
- Couscous with Tuna, Feta and Lemon Mint Dressing, 85
- Crab Étouffé, 137
- Portuguese Rice with Clams, 180
- Salade Niçoise, 78
- Salmon, Spinach and Sweet Potato Frittata, 38
- Salmon and Leek Pot Pie, 144
- Spanish Noodles, 169
- Tuna and Olive Rotini, 156

peppers, chile
- Creamy Crab and Poblano Soup, 60
- Curried Scrambled Eggs and Crab, 39
- Fish Tacos, 104
- Jamaican Crab and Okra Curry (variation), 147
- Louisiana Clams and Corn, 136
- Thai Coconut Crab Soup, 59
- Thai Tuna Salad, 74
- Tuna Taco Salad, 73

pickles and relishes (as ingredient)
- Indian Tuna Salad, 67
- Retro Tuna Salad Pasta, 84
- Salmon Salad, Classic, 68
- Vintage Tuna Salad, 64

pies, 140–46
Portuguese Rice with Clams, 180
potatoes
- Clam Pie, 142
- Creamy Crab and Poblano Soup, 60
- Italian Tuna, Potato and Green Bean Salad, 76
- Manhattan Clam Chowder, 53
- New England Clam Chowder, 52
- Salade Niçoise, 78
- Salmon, Corn and Herb Chowder with Pepper Jack, 50

potatoes *(continued)*
  Salmon and Roasted Garlic Bisque with Cajun Croutons, 48
  Sardines with Roast Spuds, Smoked Paprika Oil and Lemon, 42
  Tuna Croquettes, 124

Q

quinoa
  Citrus Quinoa with Crab and Cress, 182
  Moroccan-Style Salmon Quinoa, 181

R

Retro Tuna Salad Pasta, 84
rice
  Easy Ham and Clam Jambalaya, 179
  Lemony Salmon and Asparagus Risotto, 176
  Portuguese Rice with Clams, 180
  Russian Salmon Pie, 140
  Tuna and Spinach Risotto, 178
roe, 23
Russian Salmon Pie, 140

S

Salade Niçoise, 78
salads, 63–85. *See also* vinaigrettes
salmon, 16–17. *See also specific varieties (below)*
  Classic Salmon Salad, 68
  Fishballs Braised in White Wine Tomato Basil Sauce, 174
  Jerk Salmon Sliders, 118
  Lemony Salmon and Asparagus Risotto, 176
  Moroccan-Style Salmon Quinoa, 181

Nutty Salmon and Spinach Wraps, 103
Orzo with Salmon, Asparagus and Smoked Mozzarella, 166
Russian Salmon Pie, 140
Salmon, Avocado and Red Onion Club Sandwiches, 98
Salmon, Corn and Herb Chowder with Pepper Jack, 50
Salmon and Egg Smørrebrød, 41
Salmon and Leek Pot Pie, 144
Salmon and Roasted Garlic Bisque with Cajun Croutons, 48
Salmon and Sprout Quesadillas, 107
Salmon and White Bean Soup with Oniony Croutons, 46
Salmon Loaf, 126
Salmon Picadillo, 135
Soba Noodles with Fishballs and Snow Peas, 56
Thai Curry Salmon Burgers, 120
salmon, boneless skinless
  Faux Pho, 54
  Open Sesame Salmon Burgers, 115
  Salmon, Spinach and Sweet Potato Frittata, 38
  Seafood Summer Rolls, 108
salmon, pink
  California Salmon Salad, 80
  Salmon Burgers with Honey Ginger Mayo, 116
salmon, sockeye
  Jumbo Shells Stuffed with Salmon, Ricotta and Zucchini, 164
  Pasta with Spicy Salmon and Rapini, 163
  Vintage Creamed Salmon on Toast, 99

sandwiches and wraps, 41, 87–108
sardines, 17–18
  Sardines Caprese, 77
  Sardines on Toast with Herb Drizzle, 97
  Sardines with Roast Spuds, Smoked Paprika Oil and Lemon, 42
  Sicilian-Style Sardine Pasta, 152
sausage
  Easy Ham and Clam Jambalaya (variation), 179
  Portuguese Rice with Clams, 180
Seafood Summer Rolls, 108
sesame oil (toasted)
  Crab, Watercress and Egg Drop Soup, 58
  Crabby Cakes, 121
  Jerk Salmon Sliders, 118
  Open Sesame Salmon Burgers, 115
  Thai Tuna Salad, 74
shallots
  Caesar Vinaigrette, 83
  Crabby Cakes, 121
  Louisiana Clams and Corn, 136
  Orzo with Salmon, Asparagus and Smoked Mozzarella, 166
  Spanish Noodles, 169
Shortcut Tuna Pot Pie, 146
shrimp, 23
Sicilian-Style Sardine Pasta, 152
Soba Noodles with Fishballs and Snow Peas, 56
soups, 45–60
sour cream and yogurt
  Clam, Bacon and Chive Dip, 35
  Fish Tacos, 104
  Minty Cucumber Dip, 121, 124
  Salmon and Sprout Quesadillas, 107
  Tuna Taco Salad, 73

Spaghetti with Clam Sauce
  Two Ways, 170
Spanish Noodles, 169
spinach
  Nutty Salmon and Spinach
    Wraps, 103
  Salmon, Spinach and Sweet
    Potato Frittata, 38
  Tuna and Bean Salad on
    Arugula (variation), 72
  Tuna and Spinach Risotto,
    178
sprats, 18
sprouts
  Anchovy Egg Salad, Tomato
    and Sprouts in Pitas, 102
  Faux Pho, 54
  Salmon and Sprout
    Quesadillas, 107
squid, 23

T

Thai Coconut Crab Soup,
  59
Thai Curry Salmon Burgers,
  120
Thai Tuna Salad, 74
tinned fish. *See* canned fish
Today's Tuna Noodle
  Casserole, 130
tomatoes. *See also* tomato
  sauces; *specific types of
  tomato (below)*
  Anchovy Egg Salad, Tomato
    and Sprouts in Pitas, 102
  CBLT, 100
  Couscous with Tuna, Feta
    and Lemon Mint Dressing,
    85
  Curried Scrambled Eggs
    and Crab, 39
  Easy Ham and Clam
    Jambalaya, 179
  Fishballs Braised in White
    Wine Tomato Basil Sauce,
    174
  Fish Tacos, 104
  Louisiana Clams and Corn,
    136

Manhattan Clam Chowder,
  53
Pan Bagnat, 93
Retro Tuna Salad Pasta
  (variation), 84
Salade Niçoise, 78
Sardines Caprese, 77
Spaghetti with Clam Sauce
  Two Ways, 170
Spanish Noodles, 169
Tortellini Toss-Up, 160
Tuna Pantry Pasta, 158
Tuna Taco Salad, 73
Vintage Tuna Mac and
  Cheese, 157
tomatoes, cherry/grape
  Pasta with Tuna, Beans,
    Sage and Olives, 155
  Thai Tuna Salad, 74
  Tuna Cobb Salad, 71
  The Ziti Caper, 162
tomatoes, sun-dried
  Italian Tuna Salad, 66
  Tuna and Bean Salad on
    Arugula, 72
tomato sauces (as ingredient)
  Crab Louis, 69
  Faux Pho, 54
  Jumbo Shells Stuffed with
    Salmon, Ricotta and
    Zucchini, 164
  Niçoise Tuna Burgers, 112
  Salmon and Sprout
    Quesadillas, 107
  Salmon Picadillo, 135
Tortellini Toss-Up, 160
tortillas and tortilla chips
  Fish Tacos, 104
  Nutty Salmon and Spinach
    Wraps, 103
  Salmon and Sprout
    Quesadillas, 107
  Tuna Taco Salad, 73
tuna, 14–15
tuna, oil-packed
  Couscous with Tuna, Feta
    and Lemon Mint Dressing,
    85
  Deviled Eggs with Tuna,
    37

Italian Tuna, Potato and
  Green Bean Salad, 76
Pan Bagnat, 93
Salade Niçoise, 78
Thai Tuna Salad, 74
Tortellini Toss-Up, 160
Tuna, Egg and Fresh Bean
  Salad, 75
Tuna and Artichoke Panini,
  96
Tuna and Bean Salad on
  Arugula, 72
Tuna and Olive Rotini,
  156
Tuna and Spinach Risotto,
  178
Tuna Cobb Salad, 71
Tuna Pantry Pasta, 158
Tuna Tapenade, 32
The Ziti Caper, 162
tuna, water-packed
  Coconut Tuna and Pea
    Curry, 149
  Diner Tuna Melts, 88
  Fish Tacos, 104
  Niçoise Tuna Burgers, 112
  Parmesan Tuna
    Sandwiches, 95
  Pasta with Tuna, Beans,
    Sage and Olives, 155
  Retro Tuna Salad Pasta,
    84
  Shortcut Tuna Pot Pie, 146
  Today's Tuna Noodle
    Casserole, 130
  Tuna à la King, 134
  Tuna Croquettes, 124
  Tuna Fettuccine Alfredo,
    161
  Tuna McMelts, 89
  Tuna Muffuletta
    Sandwiches, 90
  Tuna Salad Three Ways,
    66
  Tuna Taco Salad, 73
  Tuna Tetrazzini, 132
  Tuscan Tuna Rolls, 94
  Vintage Tuna Mac and
    Cheese, 157
  Vintage Tuna Salad, 64

V

vegetables (mixed). *See also* greens; *specific vegetables*
  Easy Ham and Clam Jambalaya, 179
  Jumbo Shells Stuffed with Salmon, Ricotta and Zucchini, 164
  Manhattan Clam Chowder, 53
  Salmon, Spinach and Sweet Potato Frittata, 38

vegetables *(continued)*
  Salmon and White Bean Soup with Oniony Croutons, 46
  Shortcut Tuna Pot Pie, 146

vinaigrettes
  Caesar Vinaigrette, 83
  Homemade French Dressing, 71
  Olive Dressing, 93
  Vinaigrette, 79

Vintage Creamed Salmon on Toast, 99
Vintage Tuna Mac and Cheese, 157
Vintage Tuna Salad, 64

W

watercress
  Citrus Quinoa with Crab and Cress, 182
  Crab, Watercress and Egg Drop Soup, 58
  Salmon Burgers with Honey Ginger Mayo, 116
  Seafood Summer Rolls, 108
  Tuna Cobb Salad, 71

wine and sherry
  Catalan Clams and Ham, 36
  Clam Carbonara, 173
  Deviled Crab, 138
  Fishballs Braised in White Wine Tomato Basil Sauce, 174
  Manhattan Clam Chowder, 53
  Salmon and Leek Pot Pie, 144
  Sicilian-Style Sardine Pasta, 152
  Spaghetti with Clam Sauce Two Ways, 170
  Tuna and Spinach Risotto, 178
  Tuna Tetrazzini, 132

Y

yogurt. *See* sour cream and yogurt

Z

The Ziti Caper, 162